Recollections

of

An Old 52nd Man

RECOLLECTIONS

OF

AN OLD 52ND MAN

BY

CAPTAIN JOHN DOBBS

LATE 52ND LIGHT INFANTRY

The Spellmount Library of Military History

SPELLMOUNT
Staplehurst

British Library Cataloguing in Publication Data:
A catalogue record for this book is available
from the British Library

Copyright © Spellmount 2000
Introduction © Ian Fletcher 2000

ISBN 1-86227-093-7

First published in 1863

This edition first published in the UK in 2000
in
The Spellmount Library of Military History
by
Spellmount Limited
The Old Rectory
Staplehurst
Kent TN12 0AZ
United Kingdom

Tel: 01580 893730
Fax: 01580 893731
E-mail: enquiries@spellmount.com
Website: www.spellmount.com

1 3 5 7 9 8 6 4 2

Printed in Great Britain by
T.J. International Ltd
Padstow, Cornwall

AN INTRODUCTION
By Ian Fletcher

There is little doubt as to the identity of the first British officer casualty of the Peninsular War. That dubious distinction lies with Lieutenant Ralph Bunbury, of the 95th Rifles, who lost his life in a skirmish close to Brilos on 15 August 1808, two days before the Battle of Roliça. But who was the last officer to join the long list of casualties that accumulated during the next six years? Well, Captain John Dobbs has a remarkably solid claim, for he was badly wounded by one of the last shots fired during the final action of the war at Bayonne, on 14 April 1814. True, others died of their wounds afterwards but these had been wounded earlier in the fight. Dobbs, however, was almost certainly the last officer actually to fall. The story of John Dobbs is contained within the pages of this extremely rare book, *Recollections of an Old 52nd Man*, of which this is the second edition, which was first published in 1863.

During the last few years there has been a profusion of facsimile editions of rare memoirs, written by Wellington's men, the original editions of which fetch high prices in the antiquarian book market. But no matter how rare they are, first editions still turn up regularly in the pages of the various catalogues issued by booksellers. The same cannot be said of *Recollections of an Old 52nd Man*, however, which drew a complete blank amongst the foremost dealers when asked whether they had ever heard of it. Indeed, it has even escaped the very extensive bibliographies by Howard and Sandler, while there are no references to it in the bibliographies found in the works of such luminaries as Oman, Fortescue, Glover or Weller. It is, therefore, extremely rare and is, perhaps, the ultimate in rare books. This, naturally, is the cue for a succession of Dobbs' owners to come forward and declare their ownership of a copy, which is always the case when making such a statement. Nevertheless, it is one of the rarest memoirs I have come across in over twenty years of research into the Peninsular War. Possibly the fact that the book was printed in Ireland rather than England may have something to do with its rarity. Of course, being a rare book is one thing, but it is quite another to have the advantage of being both interesting and informative. Dobbs' *Recollections of an Old 52nd Man* has both of these qualities and, whilst it is a relatively short memoir, it nevertheless has much to add to our knowledge of the period and of life in the British Army of the early nineteenth century.

John Dobbs was only seven years old when, in 1798, he first experienced armed conflict. The Dobbs family lived in Dublin at the time of the Irish Rebellion and so bore witness to the events that unfolded around them, events that forced his father, four brothers, uncle and four cousins to take up arms in defence of Ireland. It was to be a further seven years before John Dobbs was able to take up arms himself when, at the tender age of fifteen, he was given a lieutenancy in the Armagh Militia. However, it was when he received his commission in the 52nd (Oxfordshire) Light Infantry that his military career can be said to have really begun.

Dobbs' career in the British Army embraced three of the main campaigns fought by the army between 1808 and 1814. These were Sir John Moore's expedition to Sweden in 1808, the Walcheren Campaign of 1809 and, of course, the Peninsular War, from 1808 to 1814, in which John Dobbs was a participant almost from beginning to end. His experiences in the Peninsular War form the core of his recollections and the ten clasps he received on his General Service Medal are ample proof of the extent of his services. Indeed, only three other officers of this very distinguished regiment, John Cross, William Royds and Charles Yorke gained a similar number. The clasps were awarded to Dobbs for his participation in the battles and sieges of Corunna, Fuentes de Oñoro, Ciudad Rodrigo, Badajoz, Salamanca, Vittoria, Pyrenees, San Sebastian, Nivelle and the Nive. However, not all of these clasps were awarded for actions fought whilst serving with the 52nd, because on 1 September 1813, Dobbs was given command of a company of the 5th Caçadores in the Portuguese Army. This explains why Dobbs was at Bayonne in April 1814 instead of Toulouse, which is where the 52nd were at the time, having taken part in the last major battle of the war on 10 April 1814.

With such a profusion of British Napoleonic memoirs, it is only natural that some of them are dull, tedious and often hard work to read. After all, not every memoir can be exciting and as enjoyable as the classics, such as Kincaid, Sherer or Cooper, all of which form part of this Spellmount Library of Military History.

However, even within the most dull of memoirs, which this is not, there is often a brief reference that sheds new light on a hitherto unknown fact. Amongst the many interesting things which Dobbs mentions in his memoir is the fact that only half of his company of Caçadores were armed with Baker rifles, the others having ordinary muskets. This certainly disproves the accepted view today, where countless books on military dress would have us believe that the Caçadores were armed exclusively with rifles. Once again, we have a memoir that, in spite of its relative brevity, has one or two important references that are like keys, unlocking further secrets and shedding new light on hitherto unknown or misinterpreted facts. It merely demonstrates the fact that, no matter how much we think we know about Wellington's army, I believe we will never fully understand its workings, as long as memoirs such as Dobbs' continue to yield such references. It is almost as though Wellington's veterans are mocking us from Valhalla, feeding us snippets every once and a while, just to disprove hitherto believed theories. The study of military dress, for example, is fraught with pitfalls, for with so few surviving examples of original costume it is almost impossible to discover what Wellington's men actually wore. True, we have dress regulations, but judging from the many memoirs written by Wellington's men what was set down and what was actually worn were often two very different things. Many would have us believe that grey trousers were the norm, for example. But, again, we have a reference from Dobbs to white trousers, and even these were stained blue by the dye that ran from his blue gloves when wet. It all goes to show that no matter how many new memoirs are discovered and published, I believe that there will always be a new piece of the jigsaw to put into place, although how near we are actually to finishing the puzzle heaven only knows.

The reference to Dobbs' blue trousers is contained in a paragraph in which he mentions the presence of the great Peninsular War artist, Colonel Thomas Staunton St Clair who, by happy coincidence, was also commanding officer of the 5th Caçadores. St Clair was a British officer who, like Dobbs himself, served with the Portuguese Army. In fact, St Clair served with the 21st Portuguese Line Regiment as well. His military career in the Peninsula was relatively unspectacular, but it is his paintings that have made him so famous today. Anyone who has seen his wonderful paintings contained within his *Series of Views of the Principal Occurrence of the Campaign in Spain and Portugal*, will not have failed to have appreciated the accuracy of his work. They depict with wonderful accuracy the landscape, the actions and, of course, military dress. St Clair could only paint what he saw, of course, and thus, we have the old stove-pipe shakos in his paintings, rather than the later Belgictype shakos, depicted by other artists who also painted Peninsular scenes but only after the war had ended. Indeed, St Clair, in my view, should be regarded as one of the prime sources of military art for the campaign. In many ways, he was the equivalent of a 'war artist' or even a photographer in today's conflicts. His painting of the camp at Villa Velha, close to the traditional crossing point over the Tagus, is a wonderful study of British army life in the Peninsula, full of detail and accurate scenery. It is almost possible to locate the very spot today where he painted his picture all those years ago, such is the accuracy and detail included in the painting. Dobbs mentions the fact that St Clair had included him in a picture of the action in front of Bidart, during the Battle of the Nive in December 1813, and mentions that his blue trousers were included also. The irony is that this particular painting is not included in the final twelve that were published in his *Series of Views*. If it had been, we would presumably have seen John Dobbs, complete with dyed blue trousers. I am unaware of the whereabouts, or even the existence, of the original paintings but it would be interesting to see that such a painting was done and whether Dobbs really was included in it.

The 52nd (Oxfordshire) Light Infantry was one of the regiments that formed the Light Division in the Peninsula. The division was just still a brigade in the summer of 1809 when it returned to Spain following its return from the country after the ill-fated Corunna campaign the previous winter. The Light Brigade, as it then was, was commanded by one of the British Army's great characters, Robert 'Black Bob' Craufurd, so named on account of his often violent temper. Craufurd commanded the brigade during the Corunna campaign and again during the summer of 1809. However, after the Battle of Talavera he was given command of the 3rd Division after its original commander, Mackenzie, was killed. The following February saw the arrival in the Peninsula of another great firebrand, Sir Thomas Picton. As the great Welshman was senior to Craufurd, Wellington saw fit to give command of the division to him. Craufurd naturally enough was in need of a command and so the Light Brigade was removed from the 3rd Division and, with the addition of another brigade of light troops, the Light Division was created. It was during the spring and summer of 1810 that Craufurd and his division enjoyed their period of greatest fame, manning the Portuguese–Spanish border, a total of 400 square miles, in the face of a greatly numerically superior French force. And yet, not once was Craufurd's chain of outposts pierced by the French. It was a great achievement. But it was not without its share of calamities. At Villar de Puerco, on 11 July 1810, Craufurd bungled an opportunity of capturing a French foraging party of around 200 men, whilst a far more serious affair occurred on 24 July when he almost lost the Light Division when attacked by Marshal Ney on the Coa river. Sadly, Dobbs had been sent to Walcheren, and so nothing new is learned of the Light Division's activities at this time.

Dobbs finally arrived in the Peninsula in time for Masséna's retreat from Portugal in the spring of 1811, and one of the highlights in the book includes his account of the famous action at Sabugal, on 3 April 1811. It was the final battle in Masséna's long and tortuous retreat that had seen Wellington driving the French steadily from Portugal ever since their withdrawal from their positions in front of the Lines of Torres Vedras in early March. Marshal Ney had fought successful rearguard actions at Pombal, Redinha and Cazal Nova, before coming unstuck at Foz d'Arouce on 15 March. However, none of these was as severe as the fight at Sabugal, during which the Light Division single-handedly took on Reynier's corps, in the midst of a thick fog. This was not through any design on the part of Wellington but was due to the fact that, in the fog, the division lost its way and instead of moving against the French rear, took it in the flank. There ensued a fierce seesaw struggle, during which Beckwith's brigade captured an enemy howitzer that soon became the centre of the fight. The 43rd and 95th were most actively engaged until Drummond's brigade, including the 52nd, arrived on the scene to turn the tide in favour of the Allies. The howitzer remained in possession of the Light Division but such is inter-regimental rivalry that a fierce dispute as to which regiment actually secured the gun ensued. In fact, the dispute was almost as bad as the fight itself. It is strange that the battle was not designated as a battle honour. But, then again, the powers that be had a strange way of deciding what would and would not be designated as such.

John Dobbs' story is full of the sort of exciting adventures you would expect of a young subaltern who was still only twenty-three years old at the end of the war. Nevertheless, campaign life was hard and one wonders what effect the loss of his brother, Joseph, killed at the storming of Ciudad Rodrigo on 19 January 1812, had on him. In only his twenty-first year at the time, John must have been devastated at the loss of his brother, although it is mentioned only briefly. Perhaps the loss was still painful even after the passing of many years, or perhaps it was simply the case that so many lives were lost that young men just became inured to the regular loss of life.

Ciudad Rodrigo, in fact, was one of two great sieges in which John Dobbs took part. At Ciudad Rodrigo he was there with the 52nd, storming the Lesser Breach, whilst away to his right, Henry Mackinnon's brigade of the 3rd Division attacked the Greater Breach. Both attacks were successful although, as we have seen, Dobbs' brother Joseph was killed in the attempt. Robert Craufurd was killed during the attack also, as was Mackinnon. Unperturbed, John Dobbs was again with his regiment, three months later, when it was time to storm the forbidding walls of Badajoz, the formidable and powerfully defended fortress that had denied Wellington the previous summer. When Wellington's infantry attacked the breaches on the memorable night of 6 April, a combination of brave, tenacious defenders and a series of savage and deadly obstacles again denied them. Indeed, it is estimated that some forty separate attacks took place, all of which were beaten back by a deadly cocktail of mines, musketry and grapeshot. But whilst the 4th and Light Divisions were being cast into the inferno at the breaches, the 3rd Division successfully escaladed the walls of the alcazabar, whilst Leith's 5th Division performed an equally heroic feat by climbing the walls of the San Vincente bastion. With these two divisions inside the town, French resistance at the breaches ceased, although it was still impossible to pass through the breaches until daylight, when the obstacles were dragged away. Dobbs was present at San Sebastian but only after the town had fallen on 31 August 1813. Nevertheless, the French garrison still had to be prised from the castle on top of Monte Orgullo, where they held on until 7 September.

During the Battle of the Nive in December 1813, John Dobbs was struck in the breast by a musket ball but, much to the shock – and delight – of his men, rose up, uninjured. This apparently left him with a reputation as being invulnerable, although Dobbs himself said, this was due to the thick braid on his jacket and to the silk handkerchief inside it. Nevertheless, Dobbs appears to have been saddled with the reputation and, considering the actions in which he had taken part, he does appear to have been fortunate. So, it must have come as quite a shock when, during the French sortie from Bayonne on 14 April 1814, he was badly wounded by a musket ball that struck him in the shin. 'Suddenly I felt a blow on the shin, and on looking down, found that a ball had entered between the two bones, carrying in a piece of the trowsers, which I believe was the last shot fired.' He must have cursed his luck, for the war was as good as over. Indeed, Napoleon had already abdicated, whilst the last major action of the war, at Toulouse, had been fought some four days earlier. Hence Dobbs' claim to be the last British officer to be wounded in action in the Peninsula. It is a shame that Dobbs missed out on fighting at Waterloo, as he had been promoted to the 2nd Battalion of the 52nd. Otherwise, he would, no doubt, have been present with Sir John Colborne and the first battalion of the regiment when it dealt Napoleon's Imperial Guard such a deadly blow on 18 June 1815.

When Dobbs published his fascinating little book in 1863, he was governor of Waterford District Lunatic Asylum. No doubt he had met characters in Wellington's army who gave him great experience at dealing with the inmates. After all, one would appear to have been completely mad even to think of attacking the breaches at Badajoz, for example. Nevertheless, he no doubt reflected on these past years with some pride and satisfaction, which is probably why he was moved to write his book. Dobbs no doubt took advantage of the six volume *History of the War in the Peninsula* that had been written by William Napier, who, like Dobbs, had also served in the Light Division. Napier's great work appeared between 1828 and 1845, which gave Dobbs ample time and opportunity to draw upon them. Indeed, some of Napier's writings are quoted. However, Dobbs appear not to have been too unduly influenced by Napier, unlike some other memoirs that quote wholesale from him. Instead, we have a first-class memoir, full of the personal experience of battle and a worthy addition to The Spellmount Library of Military History.

Ian Fletcher,
Rochester, 2000

RECOLLECTIONS

OF

AN OLD 52ND. MAN;

BY

CAPT. JOHN DOBBS,

(LATE 52ND LIGHT INFANTRY)

SECOND EDITION.

———◆———

WATERFORD :

PRINTED BY JOHN S. PALMER, 49, LADY LANE.

———

1863.

PREFACE.

THE publication of the 52nd Record by Captain Moorram having enabled me to ascertain some dates and places in which my memory failed, I have availed myself of it in this edition, and added some other matter which may be found interesting to its readers.

J. D.

WATERFORD,
9th July, 1863.

CONTENTS.

CHAPTER IV.

CHAPTER V.

CHAPTER VI.

CONCLUSION.

INTRODUCTION.

My father, Francis Dobbs, Esq., barrister-at-law, and member of Parliament, was descended from an officer of rank in Queen Elizabeth's army, who settled in the North of Ireland, and married a gran'daughter of O'Neill, Earl of Tyrone. My father was rather remarkable as a public character. He took an active part in the politics of his day, as a writer, and as a speaker in the House of Commons; also, in the "Irish Volunteers," being reviewing Major to Lord Charlemont. He neglected his profession for these public matters to the injury of his private affairs. My mother, daughter of Alexander Stuart, of Ballintoy, a branch of the Bute family, was left a widow, with very limited means, when I was ten years old. We then resided in Dublin.

The first public event which made an impression on me was the Irish rebellion of 1798. I was then seven years old. Four hundred thousand united Irishmen were banded together for the overthrow of the British Government in Ireland, and had promises of assistance from the French Government, who had attempted to land fifteen thousand men at Bantry Bay in 1796, but were prevented by a violent storm. In 1798 the rebellion broke out, and the French sent another fleet, with three thousand five hundred men, who were to land in the North of Ireland. This fleet was defeated by Sir John B. Warren; most of the ships were taken. Another fleet succeeded in landing nine hundred men at Kilala; they advanced into the interior, and were defeated at Ballynamuck by our troops. At this time the defence of Ireland depended on her Militia (and some of the Southern regiments were not to be depended on, having a number of sworn rebels in them) and corps of Yomanry, which were formed wherever a suf-cient body of loyal subjects could be collected. Their number was 82,941, of which 11,000 were cavalry—they were principally from the Northern counties. In Dublin there were the Lawyers, Attorneys, Merchants, and College Corps, and several others, amongst which, one called Beresford's, bore a prominent part. The loyal male members of every family were attached to one of them; and on the ringing of the alarm bells, and the drums beating to arms, each repaired to the alarm post of his corps, leaving the women and children in a state of anxiety.

My father, four brothers, uncle, and four first cousins, were at this time under arms for the defence of Ireland. My brother William commanded a company of the Armagh Militia at Ballynamuck, and my brother Francis was engaged with the Lisburn Yeomanry at Ballynahinch.

On the 1st August, 1798, Nelson attacked the French fleet, consisting of 13 sail of the line, and some smaller vessels, with twelve British ships of the line in the Nile, and after a bloody engagement took nine of them, and burnt two more. He also captured two frigates, and a number of gun boats. In Dublin the rejoicings for this victory were most enthusiastic; every house was illuminated from top to bottom. It was a grand sight. Splendid transparancies were to be seen in every direction, and the streets were crowded by all classes, in their best attire.

In 1806 Nelson's destruction of the combined fleets of France and Spain, off Trafalgar, put an end to Boneparte's hopes of invading England, his fleets being all but annihilated. He had prepared, at Boulgne, for the above purpose, a camp of one hundred and sixty thousand men, and an immense flotilla of flat-bottomed boats and gun-boats. These boats were to have been rowed across during the first heavy fog. At this time Bonaparte's allies included all the continental powers with the exception of Sweden.

In the same year, I being fifteen years old, Lord Gosford gave me a Lieutenancy in the Armagh Militia, in which my brother Francis was Captain. I joined them at Ennis, in the County Clare, whence we marched to Tuam, in Galway, when I had some hard night duty, "still hunting." We had a Subaltren's guard here, and the guard-room was infested with rats. While sleeping on the guard bed, I was awakened by a troop of them making off with the candle which was lighting on the table.

We were then sent to Eyrcourt, leaving detachments at Banagher and Shannon Bridge, at which places I was successively stationed. While here, our men were trained to the great guns in the batteries. During my stay at

Shannon Bridge, my brother and I visited Ballinasloe during the great fair held there, and were witnesses to a great faction fight. There was a large body on each side, and they fought with sticks and stones to the terror of all persons peacably inclined. All the shops were closed, shutters put up, and business suspended. Such was the state of most of the large towns in Ireland, and it continued so till after Peel's Act for the establishment of the present police. Soon afterwards we were removed to Naas, near Dublin, where I received my appointment to the 52nd (Sir John Moore being an old schoolfellow of my fathers), in which regiment my brother Joseph was a captain. Having gone out in the expedition to Ferrol as a volunteer, he distinguished himself in boarding a Spanish vessel, in consequence of which he received his commission in the 52nd. His services in the 52nd will be mentioned in my recollections of that corps. My brother Alexander entered the Navy, and after many boat services he particularly distinguished himself on the lakes of Canada. In the capture of Oswago, and Fort Erie, on which lake we had not an armed vesssel, while the Americans had three armed schooners with a crew of 35 men each, being 105 men, and 92 lbs of metal. They were anchored off the Fort, a short distance above the falls of Niagara in a position calculated to prevent its attack by our troops.

My brother, who was in command of the *Charwell* and *Nancy* below the falls of Niagara, took 75 of his men and gig, which they landed below the fall, at Queenstown, carrying it for twenty miles on their shoulders, and launched it into Lake Erie, at Frenchman's Creek, where he procured five batteaux with which he succeeded in boarding and carrying two of the schooners. The third, by cutting her cable, got away, leaving the boats struggling with the rapids above the fall, from which they had a narrow escape. He then assisted the troops in the capture of the fort. Afterwards receiving a wound in the head,—the effects of which hastened his death. For his services at Fort Erie he was made C.B., and Posted, he being only a commander in command of the fleet on Lake Erie. My brother William had a company in the Armagh Militia, and distinguished himself during the rebellion in the action in Ballynamuck. He died from

fever, contracted while on guard at Kilmainham. My
brother Francis volunteered from the Armagh Militia
with one hundred men just before the peace, and got a
company in the 12th Foot, but was reduced to half pay
before the period, when it would have become permanent.

The 52d regiment was employed in North America from
1765 to 1778, taking a distinguished part in the battle
of Bunker's Hill, and the various operations with the
United States; in India from 1783 to 1796, taking
a distinguished part in the operations which led to the
conquest of the Misore and the island of Ceylon.

In 1799 they got a second battalion, and 1800 both
battalions were employed in the expedition to Ferrol, in
which they took an active part in what little was done;
in 1803 the 2nd battalion was made the 96th Regiment,
and the 1st battalion made light infantry, being the
picked men of both battalions. In 1804 a 2nd battalion
was again added from 1803 to 1808; the 1st battalion
was employed in Cicily.

In 1807 the 2nd battalion was employed in taking
Copenhagan, and the Danish fleet which Buonaparte
was about employing against us.

The 1st battalion embarked for Sweeden on the 30th
of April 1808, and arrived at Gottenburg on the 17th
May, from whence it sailed for England on the 3rd of
July, and arrived at Spithead on the 21st August. The 2nd
battalion had preceeded the 1st embarking on the 16th
July, and landing in Portugal on the 19th of August, took
an active part in the Battle of Vimiera on the 21st.

The 1st battalion sailed from Corunna on the 17th
January, 1809, and arrived in England on the 25th.

The 2nd battalion sailed from Viga on the 13th January, and landed at Ramsgate the end of the month.

The 1st battalion again embarked for Portugal on the
25th of May, 1809, and landed at Lisbon on the 5th of
July, and joined Lord Wellington's army at Talavera
after a forced march of sixty-two miles in twenty-six
hours, and served in the Peninsula up to the end of the
war.

The origin of the 52nd regiment, dated from the eve
of the commencement of the contest known in history as
the Seven Years' War, the French having raised a pow-

erful navy, the peace of Aix-la-Chapelle was soon broken,
and in the winter of 1755 the attack made by them in
the British settlement beyond the Alleghany Mountains
in North America hastened the crisis, when, therefore,
war between the two countries was inevitable; an aug-
mentation was made to the army, and in December, 1755,
eleven regiments of infantry were raised, which have
since been retained, and numbered from the 50th to the
60th inclusive, becoming part of the celebrated light division covering the retreat to the lines, and taking a
prominent part in the battle of Busaco, defence of the
lines of Tores Vedras, advance after Massenas retreating
army, combat of Sabugal, battle of Fuentes D'Onor,
seiges of Rodrigo and Badajos, battle of Salamanca,
taking of Madrid and covering the Burgas retreat, advance and taking of Burgas affair at St. Milan and battle of Victoria, battles of the Pyrenees, storming the
heights of Vera, battles of Nivell, Nive, Orthes and
Toulouse in 1814.

In 1816, although the regiment did not get credit fon
it in the Duke's dispatch after the battle of Waterloo, i⁻
is now ascertained, without contradiction, that the de⁻
feat of the young guard was by the 52nd Regiment under
Lord Seaton, and the total route of the French army the
result.   It bears on its colors :—

HINDOSTAN,	VITTORIA,
VIMIERA,	NIVELLE
CORUNNA,	NIVE,
BUSACO,	ORTHES,
FUENTES D'ONOR	TOULOUSE,
CUIDAD RODRIGO,	PENINSULA
BADAJOS.	WATERLOO.
SALAMANCA,	

" A regiment never surpassed in arms since arms were
first borne by men.— *W. Napier Nevelle*, 1813.

The junior veterans of the Peninsular War have to
thank a 52nd man for their services being recognised by
Her Majesty.   While the Duke of Wellington opposed
the medal, and all the inferior officers who had themselves been decorated, backed him or hung back.   The
Duke of Richmond stood out and maintained their cause
and the medal was granted on the 1st of June, 1847, after
many of them had ceased to exist, and thirty-three years

after it terminated, at which time I received a medal and ten clasps for Corunna, Fuentes d'Omor, Cudad Rodrigo, Badajoz, Salamanca, Vittoria, Pyrrenees, St. Sabastion, Nevelle, and Nive.

While we, the left wing under Sir John Hope, protected the flank of the main army from 15,000 picked troops behind the walls of Bayonne, they got clasps for Orthes and Toulouse, while we got none, although engaged for fifty days and nights, which ended in a sortee, in which we lost Sir John Hope (taken prisoner), Gen. Hay killed and Sir Thomas Bradford wounded before it was driven back to its ramparts, and I was severely wounded by the last shot fired, and I believe the last shot fired in that war

RECOLLECTIONS

OF

AN OLD 52ND MAN.

CHAPTER I.

Join the 52nd Regiment—Its drill—Expedition to
Sweden—Sail to the Peninsula—Landing in Portugal
—Funeral, Indulgences—Bell christened—Army re-
ligion—March to Spain—A Spanish welcome—Ad-
vance of Buonaparte—A night march—Retreat of the
British Army—Battle of Corunna—Death of Sir John
Moore—Embarkation—Arrival in Englang.

On joining the 52nd Regiment, in 1808, I found myself in the midst of perfect gentlemen.   The duty was
carried on like clock work, and scarcely any wine drank
at the mess, frequently none.   After dinner we used to
spend the evening playing foot-ball, rackets, &c.; we
had constant roll-calls for eye washing; every man was paraded with the lid of his camp-cattle full of water which
they washed them with. I was not allowed to take command
of a section going to church till I finished my drill. In drill
every man was taught his centre of gravity by the balance step,—to take an exact length of pace by the pace
stick,— to step in slow, quick and double quick,
by the plummet and tap of the drum, afterwards to
move in bodies or extended order and out post duty, &c.

The officers having to go through every part of it, the
drill was brought to such perfection that a line of 1000
men has been known to march over Shorncliff without
any perceptible departure from their dressing.
Shortly after I had been dismissed from drill the regi-

ment joined Sir John Moore's expedition to Sweden, and
I take this opportunity to mention some of the disad-
vantages we then laboured under. We had no marching
money, no prince's allowance or sea-stock provided, and
had to lay in our own. We were obliged to prepare
for a much longer period than the voyage was likely to
last, from the uncertainity of sailing vessels; a voyage
which could now be performed in a day, at that time
frequently occupied weeks.

The vessel I embarked in was an old merchantman, of
about two hundred tons, called the "Three Brothers,"
Reynett and Dobbs companies, two hundred strong, with
seven officers, were its occupants. The cabin had two
births on each side, one over the other—these were of
course chosen by the four seniors, while the three juniors
slept in cots swung to the ceiling, and only a few inches
apart. They were afterwards increased to nine, the two
added placed the two juniors on the floor, one on each
side of the table which was in the centre. The first thing
to be done by our servants was to remove the five move-
able beds, and after we had washed to arrange the cabin
for breakfast the table was lashed to the floor. In a gale
of wind one day, the lashing gave way while we were at
dinner, and threw Captain Reynett (now Lieut. General
Sir John) against the bulkhead, emptying a tureen of
peasoup on his head, which was the cause of some amusement to those who escaped the disaster, and our catirer,
(now Sir T. E. Drake) also gave us a laugh by the way
he recommended the ration pork, pressing each number
of the mess to partake of it, till at last some of us observed that he never eat any himself, and he was asked why,
in answer to which, he said, my good fellows, my mother
told me never to make a beast of myself. The plan in
the 52nd was to laugh each other out of any eccentricities
we observed, and accordingly we attacked Maitland about
his going over each dish commenting on the manner it
was cooked, and they certainly would not bear compari-
son with what he sat down to, at Lord Londerdale's, his
father. We remained in the Three Brothers during our
stay in Sweden, and until our arrival on the coast of
Portugal, where we landed the day after the battle of
Vimiero. The vessel proceeded with our baggage to the

Tagus, where she took in a shipful of French troops, sent home by the convention of Cintra. Shortly after leaving the Tagus, she foundered Having encoutered very rough weather in the Baltic Sea, English Channel, and Bay of Biscay, we had a fortunate escape.

On our way to Sweden we had to pass the Skagerrack in a dense fog, and against a head wind, while a large fleet were all tacking, so that it was next to impossible to escape collision. We had drums beating, bugles blowing, bells ringing, and men shouting, having to avoid the enemy's shore on our right hand, and rocky islands on our left.

We arrived at Gottenburgh on the 17th May, 1808, and returned to England in the beginning of July.

While lying in Gottenbrugh harbour, we were rather surprised to find the body of one of our men, who had been drowned bathing, after a length of time rising at the same spot. It appears there are no tides in the Baltic; another fact peculiar to that latitude also came under notice, *and that was daylight at the hour of midnight, at the time we were there.*

These men were frequently landed for exercise on an uninhabited island (of which there were many) in the harbour, and as it was full of hares, there was often a hunt after the first one seen, which was generally succeeded by several others being started, which caused a most exciting scene, the hunters separating into as many parties as there were hares.

We also had a boats crew selected from our men, with which we could man one of the ships boats, and visit the other ships, or land on one of the islands for bathing, &c.

On one occasion my brother having dined on board one of the ships, I took the boat for him, it was blowing very fresh, and on our return came on to blow harder, so that we found it hard work to get back, and were nearly upset by getting foul of a ship's cable.

I visited Gottenburgh, but cannot remember anything about it worthy of remark, except that the general appearance was pleasing. On leaving Gottenburgh harbour, after a heavy gale of wind, we found ourselves in the midst of seven water-spouts. It was a grand sight; we passed through them without injury.

Having the morning watch while passing up the chan‑nel, from the Baltic, I was agreeably surprised by the smell of new-mown hay, We were not then in sight of the land, and it seemed particularly sweet from our hav‑ing been so long on board. Having touched at Ports‑mouth we proceeded on our way to Portugal, touching at Plymouth, and were supplied with more flatbottomed boats for landing men. We were subsequently obliged to put into Torbay from stress of weather, and it was some time before we could get out of the channel. After crossing the bay of Biscay, we got into a shoal of gurnets, it extended for a considerable distance, and could be seen at a considerable distance, and could be seen in its length and breadth, all the snouts of the fishes being above the surface, there was a number of herring hogs following and feeding on them, as the weather was calm, we were able to fish over the side catching them as fast as we could throw in our lines, we also caught some needle-fish, and at night the sea appeared to be on fire as we passed through it.

We landed near Vimera on the 22nd August. 1808, in a heavy surf, with only the clothes we wore, one blanket and a few days' provisions in our haversacks, and biavouacked in the French huts that night. These huts were branches of trees with the butts on the ground, and the tops meeting, the small branches serving for thatch

Having arrived off the coast of Portugal on the 21st August, 1808, on which day our 2nd battalion took an active part in the battle of Vimera, we got orders to land the following morning, and had to abandon any sea-stock, which we could not carry in our haversacks or canteens, and having a quantity of spruce beer, which was beginning to fly, our amusement the evening before was fixing a mark in the ceiling, and letting the corks fly at it. We attempted to land in the flat-bottomed boats, but, one or two of the first that attempted it were swamped by the surf, and the men drowned. It was therefore found necessary to use the men at war boats, and we were changed into them, in which operation I had a narrow escape of losing my leg between the two boats; I however escaped with a severe bruise, which did not prevent me marching with the regiment. Immediately after landing on the 22nd, we had to cross over several extensive vineyards, to the great delight of the troops, who helped themselves to the grapes, the roots of which are at a short distance from one another, having been bared of the old branches for firing, the new branches are covered with clusters of them, the appearance at a little distance is like that of field peas, when ripe, they are carried into houses having large shallow reservoir which they are spread over, having sufficient slope to let the juice run to a spout prepared for emptying it into casks ready for its reception. When the grapes are spread a number of persons, with not very clean feet, are sent into the reservoir, who tramp them till the juice runs off, after this, the skins are collected and put into the press, which is a coil of rope several feet high, a heavy beam moving on a pivot, being a powerful levers, presses the coil of rope till all the remaining juice is pressed out of them, the juice thus obtained, is allowed to ferment in large vessels. In Spain it is conveyed from place to place, in pigskins turned inside out, and coated with tar, they are slung on the backs of mules, whose pack saddles are well adapted for the service; when exposed to the heat of the sun, and the skins not very new, the tar and hair become blended with the wine which becomes anything but agreeable. Wine was frequently issued in place of the ration—rum, and until accustomed to it, it was considered a grand thing by the men, to be drinking wine.

To the great joy of the men, they were relieved from hair-tying which was a burden grievous to be borne. And our huts being close to those occupied by the men, we could hear them joking one another on the subject; one of the principal ones was calling on their comrade to tie them, which was impossible, as their hair was gone.

Our first days march was a short one, but the weight each man had to carry was tremendous in addition to heavy knapsacks; there were their muskets and accoutrements, seventy rounds of ammunition, a blanket, a mess kettle, and wooden canteen. They and their officers had three day's provisions. The weather was very hot; our caps and leather stocks gave us great annoyance—the former by day, and the latter, both day and night. As we slept in our clothes we remedied the former by boring two small holes in the sides, and the officers, the latter, by clasping them over the knee; the men, by slipping them over the ramrod. We, each of us, had a small tin tot which we carried with a knife and fork, made to shut up like a common clasp knife. The tot was in constant requisition. On getting up it was paraded with water to wash my mouth; at breakfast, it answered for a teacup, on the march, for drinking out of, at dinner, for soup, after dinner, for rum, punch, or wine. After some time I supplied its place with a small silver cup for the same uses; also, a silver fork, both of which, being easily cleaned, were great luxuries.

As we had no change of clothes till our arrival in Lisbon, we had to take advantage of some running stream, and wash our shirts as well as we could, sitting by till they dried. We were billeted in Lisbon for several days, and took the opportunity of visiting remarkable places about it, amongst others a gambling house greatly frequented, and were surprised to find the most active persons to be the priests and monks, some of them partners in the concern. As I passed through the streets, every corner had a woman frying and selling sardines, which appeared very plenty, and gave occupation to a great many fishermen, who had an image of their patron saint in the bow of each boat with a small begging-box under it, having a slit in the top, and lock attached. As their prayers are addressed to the saint for success in their fishing, when they are disappointed, they fly into a rage with the saint, and duck his image, giving him all sort of abuse. The key of the money box is kept by a priest, who relieves it of its contents from time to time.

Another thing which strikes a stranger is, the constant assassinations, a number of bodies being found every morning—some stabbed by enemies, others by bravoes, hired for the purpose. What applies to Lisbon is equally applicable to all the larger towns and cities in Spain and Portugal. When billitted in Oporta, at the end of the war, the native merchant on whom I was billited, told me the following anecdote which was told himself by a friend:—That, having in a fit of anger, hired a bravo to murder a friend. On becoming calm he went to the bravo's house to prevent his doing the deed. The man not being at home, he asked where he was to be found. The answer was, at church, to which he followed him, and observed him earnestly engaged in his devotions. As soon as they were over, he joined him, and after letting him know that he had changed his mind, and would not have the man murdered, he asked him how he could engage in prayer when about to commit such an act. The bravo replied that he was asking for success in the job. The weapon used for assassinations is a stilleto. It has a straight-handle and blade, the latter tappering to a point. It is carried in the slieve, and when about to use it, the handle is turned with the blade backwards along the arm, which hides it from observation. The bravo passes the person on the left side, giving him a back-stroke which strikes into the heart, he still moving on as if nothing had happened.

They are very dexterous in throwing it.   his is done by laying the handle in the palm, with the blade outward, and with a jurk discharging it up, down, or straightforward, with so certain an aim as to strike a mark of one penny piece at twelve paces distance.

The building occupied by the inquisition was not to be seen, but the inquisition itself had been suppressed by the French, not only in Lisbon, but throughout the Peninsula. In Madrid the whole system was exposed by them. All the subterranian apartments having been discovered by one of their engineers, who suspected them to be under the Chapel, he poured a quantity of water on the flags, which found its way through the joining on the flag that covered the stair cases leading to them.

It is a slur upon the English that the French have done more to suppress this dreadful institution, than the English authorities who call themselves Protestants.

The 52nd having crossed the Tagus, a little above Lisbon, marched through the Alentejo. Our first days march was distressing from want of water—not a drop being to be had from the time we started till we got into quarters for the night. The consequence was, that the men fell out by hundreds, but even this had some advantage, as they marked the road for those in the rear.

While on the advance to Estremoz, we met the French garrison of Elvas on its way to Lisbon for embarkation, as agreed on in the convention of Cintra. Having halted in this neighbourhood, an Irishman of the name of Patrick Donovan deserted to us. It appeared that he had been implicated in the Irish rebellion, and had been banished to the Continent. He said he had been made a present of to the King of Prussia, and entered his services. When that country had become subject to Buonaparte, he had been transferred to the French army, and shared in most of Buonaparte's victories. He had now made his escape with a hope of getting home to his country. He was a noble soldier; he joined my brother's company, and served through the Peninsula campaign. His experience of French tactics, and his fear of being recaptured kept him always on the alert, and when he found us careless, he would caution us to be on our guard, and always kept a sharp look out himself.

We waited till the beginning of November at Estremoz, and enjoyed the fruits of that country in all their perfection, melons, water melons, oranges, figs, grapes, and what I observed at Lisbon, as it regards Sardinas, might be observed here and elsewhere of chesnuts, every corner having stoves for roasting them. We were greatly annoyed by the constant ringing of the church bells; they never ceased. We were also surprised to find a list of sins and prohibited articles of food hung at each church door, with a price attached, for which they might be indulged in, a bell was made a Christian, and got a name. We never paraded for Protestant worship, but were paraded for a Roman Catholic ceremony, and presented arms to the host as it passed, which did not give us any concern at that time. At this place I witnessed the interment of a beautiful young female in one of the churches. She was in full dress, and was carried on a bier. A flag had been taken up and a grave dug, in which she was laid, and when a few inches of clay had been laid over her, they began to pound it with a piece of wood, made like a paving *malet*, until nearly all the earth taken out was forced back.

In the beginning of November, 1808, we entered

Spain. In the first village we had a sample of Spanish welcome; we were told that we were not wanted, that they could fight their own battles without our help, &c.

A number of houses were told off for our company's quarters, but we had great difficulty in getting in, the doors being closed against us. One of the houses appeared to be untenanted, and we were going to break the door open, when an old woman put her head out of a window over it, and then held out an old matchlock gun, in order to frighten us away, her hand shaking with age and fright. When we got to Salamanca we found a change for the better, at least I did; the old lady on whom I was billited used to send me a cup of chocolate, and a thin slice of toast every morning before I was up, and paid every attention to my comfort, while I remained with her, which was till the 11th of December, 1808.

On the 23rd we were cantoned at Schagun, after Lord Paget with his Hussars had driven the French Dragoons out of it. At this time Napoleon, with sixty thousand men, was marching from Madrid to intercept us, while Soult had thirty thousand in our front, and we were only twenty-two thousand. Sir John Moore's object was to give the Spaniard's an opportunity to rally, by drawing off the French force, but it was of no use.

On the 23rd of December, 1808, we had a night march to attack Soult. The snow lay on the ground several inches deep, and we were forbidden to speak. Unexpectedly, about midnight, the word was passed from the rear to counter-march, and we returned to our quarters. On the 25th we were in full retreat, the reserve in which the 52nd were being the rear-guard, with the exception of the Hussar Brigade, who remained behind till we entered the mountains, and then passed us.

At Benevente, Buonaparte overtook, but failed in intercepting us, when he made his appearance on the heights over the bridge, the Reserve got under arms, and drew up in front of the town, the Hussar Brigade being on the plain, between us and the river, with their picquets at the bridges and fords. On this occasion, for the first and last time, I saw Napoleon I; he had a numerous staff in attendance; but, my brother's glass being a good one, I was able to distinguish him, as he reconnoitered us.

Finding that we had slipped through his fingers, he took his departure after seeing his Imperial Guard very roughly handled by the Hussar Brigade, who were left behind while we continued our retreat. On this occasion the French lost a general and seventy prisoners, with a number of men killed and wounded.

Just before the enemy's advance to Cacabelas, the Reserve were halted on the heights above it for the purpose of hanging three marauders. Everything was ready, and a square formed round the gallows, when a hussar rode in from the rear, reporting to General Paget that the enemy was close at hand. He cooly received the report, and proceeded to address the troops, stating the disgrace attached to the crime, but that he would pardon them if they would refrain from such excess; but that, if this promise was not made, they should die, if the enemy were firing into the square. There was a general exclamation of "We will! we will!" He made a sign to the Provost Marshal, who immediately liberated the prisoners. The troops were at once moved off—some to cover the retreat on this side of the river, while others crossed and took up a position to cover their retreat over the bridges. After repulsing the enemy, the retreat was cotinued. It may be well to state that Sir John Moore snerintended the v rious operations necessary to retard the advancing enemy, taking advantage of every height and defile, placing a gun where it could tell on their advance,and throwing a schrapnel shell, so as to discharge itself into a column of Infantry or Cavalry, as required. This was our occupation by day,which delay had to be made up for at night. The want of rest made us subject to optical illusions—one remarkable one I think worthy of mention. The head of the column came to a small stream running across the road (which became magnified in their sight) to a broad river of unknown depth. The front rank halted, and, of course, all in their rear did the same, and all sat down in mud nearly knee deep, and at once fell fast asleep. Some staff officer discovered the mistake, or it is likely we should have remained till morning.

There was a great deal of suffering from dysentry, and there were prisoners taken by the enemy in consequence of men being obliged to fall out. In this the Highlanders had a great advantage over the Reserve, who wore trowsers.

As there is a prejudice against low-sized men, the fact that the lowest man in my brother's company (I don't think he was five feet three inches, men being scarce in those days) in addition to his own knapsack, carried that of our right hand man for the latter part of the retreat, who was fully six feet high, breadth making up for length. The retreat of the reserve occupied 18 days, the distance was about 230 miles. The French army under Soult, after Napoleon had left him, was sixty thousand men and ninety guns, while Sir John Moore's army only consisted of nineteen thousand, three thousand having been sent to Vigo. During the greater part of this retreat, we had to march all night and halt by day, to allow the baggage, stores, and stragglers to get off; when we moved on, the rear files of the rifle corps, and the advance files of the enemy were constantly engaged. No new hand could stand the night work; some officers who joined us on the retreat, having come out with Sir David Baird to Corunna, were so ill after the first night's exposure that they had to go back to Corunna. The roads were nearly knee deep with mud, and part of the mountain with snow. When we got to Lugo, we were relieved for the night, and occupied a convent. All the officers of the 52nd were crowded into one small room, having closed the window-shutters and door, and having a charcoal pan lighting, our adjutant, who was the first to lie down, was seized with convulsions, but being carried out immediately recovered, which shewed us the danger we had escaped, and its cause.

Having offered battle to the enemy at Lugo, our baggage was sent to the rear, and unfortunately our rations, cloaks, and blankets were on the mules, and we never saw them again. One of the men having thrown away half his blanket to lighten himself, I picked it up, and turning down a foot of the end over a string, which I tied round my neck, it answered all the purposes of a cloak. Having got a bullock's heart from one of the butchers, we had it hot and cold for breakfast, dinner, and supper, till our rations became due. It may be imagined what we suffered during the rest of our retreat, again being the

12

rear guard. Our shoes being worn out, we got some of
those sent out, I believe for Spanish troops, and these
being supplied by contract, were so bad that a few hours'
marching left them without soles. In this state we
arrived at Corunna, and were allowed to go into some
houses in the neighbourhood.

During the retreat, we were in such need of rest that
we often fell asleep whilst marching, and as I had to
carry one of the colors, the unfortunate man in my front
often suffered from the pole, whilst I, in return, frequently
knocked my head against the butt end of his musket.
None but staff officers were allowed to have horses. On
our coming in sight of Corunna no fleet was there to
convey us off, but it arrived shortly afterwards.

(Corunna and Napier, vol. 1, page 488.)

" These divisions occupied the town and suburbs, the
reserve was posted with its left at the village of El Buno
and its right on the road to St. Iago Compostello. For
twelve days these hardy soldiers had covered the retreat,
during which time they had traversed eighty miles of
road in two marches, passed several nights under arms in
the snow at the mountains, were seven times engaged
with the enemy, and they now assembled at the outposts
having fewer men missing from the ranks (including
those who had fallen in battle) than any other division
in the army. An admirable instance of the value of good
discipline, and a manifest proof of the malignant injustice
with which Sir J. Moore has been accused of precipitating
his retreat beyond the measure of human strength. On the
morning of the 16th January, 1809, the day of the battle
of Corunna, while preparing our breakfast of flour and
milk, a tremendous explosion took place, and a quantity
of matter from the roof fell into the vessels, completely
spoiling the contents. This was caused by the destruction of the powder magazine which was done to prevent
it falling into the hands of the enemy. On inspecting the
quarters, the men lay as if dead over the floors, but the
enemy had hardly fired his first gun before every man
was up and ready for action, in which they immediately
engaged.

(Napier, Vol 1, page 492 and 3.)

" The late arrival of the transports, the increasing

force of the enemy, and the disadvantageous nature of the ground augmented the difficulty and danger of the embarkation so much that several general officers proposed to the Commander-in-chief that he should negociate for leave to retire to his ships unmolested. There was little chance of such a proposal being agreed to by the enemy, and there was no reason to try. The army had suffered but not from defeat, its situation was dangerous, but far from desperate, and the General would not consent to remove the standard of energy and prudence which marked his retreat by a negociation that would have given an appearance of timidity and indecision to his previous operations as opposite to their real character as light is to darkness. His high spirit and clear judgment revolted at the idea, and he rejected the degrading advice without hesitation.

All the encumbrances of the army were shipped in the night of the 15th, and on the morning of the 16th, everything was prepared to withdraw the fighting men as soon as darkness would permit them to move without being perceived.

The British had only 14,500 infantry in position at Corunna; they had no cavalry, the men being embarked and most of the horses shot; any fit for service were embarked with 52 pieces of artillery; and eight British 6-pounders and four Spanish guns were in position at the battle. The latter were not effective, our balls not fitting.

Their position was a high range which encircled a lower one occupied by our army. Their cavalry were on the left of the French eleven-gun battery, which commenced the action.

BATTLE OF CORUNNA.

The village we occupied was about half a mile in the rear of General Hopes' division. About three o'clock they opened fire from a battery of eleven guns, which had been masked with straw. Under the cover of this fire he advanced to the attack in four columns, two of which attacked the right and centre; that on the right was met by the rifle corps, while that on the centre was received by Lord William Bentick ; Brigadier-General Paget was ordered up with the reserve in support, and

14

the 52nd ordered to relieve the rifle corps (their ammunition being expended and most of their swords out of order) which we did in extended order sending the colors to the rear. Sir Sidney Beckwith met us, calling out, "Come here with your bayonets, come here with your bayonets." Reynett's company, in which I was one of the first engaged, and the first man hit was close by me; he fell apparently dead by the ball, it having entered the forehead and passed out at the back of the head, so that I said nothing could be done for him; but what was my surprise afterwards to find he was not killed, the ball having passed round the head under the skin. On recovering his senses he was taken by some passers by to the rear and re-embarked; he was recovering of the wound when he was attacked by fever and carried off. We continued to drive the enemy before us till getting on its left flank they had to withdraw the other column, attacking our centre at the village of Elvina, and return to the strong position which they had left for the attack.

DEATH OF SIR JOHN MOORE.
(Napier, vol. 1, page 490)

" Sir John Moore, while earnestly watching the result of the fight about the village of Elvina, was struck on the left breast by a canon shot; it threw him from his horse with violence; he rose again in a sitting posture, his countenance changed, and his steadfast eye still fixed upon the regiments engaged in his front. No sigh betrayed a sensation of pain, but in a few moments when he was satisfied that the troops were gaining ground, his countenance brightened and he suffered himself to be taken to the rear. Then was seen the dreadful nature of his hurt. The shoulders were shattered to pieces, the arm was hanging by a piece of skin, the ribs over the heart broken and bared of flesh, and the muscles at the breast torn into long strips, which were interlaced by their recoil from the dragging of the shot. As the soldiers placed him in a blanket his sword got entangled, and the hilt entering the wound, Captain Hardinge, a staff officer who was near, attempted to take it off, but the dying man stopped him, saying, 'It is as well as it is; I had rather it should go out of the field with me,' and in that manner so becoming to a soldier, Moore was borne from the field."

As soon as it was dark we lighted our fires as if we were going to remain for the night, but afterwards began to move off. On getting to the beach, we found the boats waiting for us, and immediately pushed off, but lost one another in the darkness, and some of us not knowing where to find our ships got on board the first we came to, sending back the boats for others who were waiting for them. Here we had no sea stock but were provided with the usual ship rations, which in those days were of the worst description. As soon as the enemy found that we had embarked, they brought a battery of guns to play on us, and as the consequences of a raking shot in our crowded state would be very bad, we made our captain cut his cable.

While passing through the Bay of Biscay one of the guns on the quarter deck broke loose, and coming against the skylight broke all the glass, which came down to us in the cabin as we lay about the floor ; fortunately the gun was secured before it could follow the glass. The voyage was not a long one; the captain supposing he was going on shore at Beachy Head, cast anchor, when, to our agreeable surprise we found ourselves in the morning alongside the flag-ship, at Spithead, the commander of which received the first intelligence of the battle of Corunna from Captain Sparks, of the 51st, who had come in the same ship as myself.

The remainder of the fleet having arrived, I went on board our head quarter ship, and having got some money from the paymaster, I went to an hotel in Portsmouth, purchasing some articles of clothing on my way. There I went into a bed-chamber, and having procured a large tub of water, and throwing all the clothes I had worn from the commencement of the retreat out of the window. I washed myself, and putting on the new clothes experienced a sensation of comfort, not easily described. Having ordered a beef-steak for dinner, a comrade, who shared it with me, was very angry at not having oyster sauce ! Our troubles, however, were not all over, as, the day after our arrival, one of our men went into his berth and died. We were ordered to Ramsgate to disembark, before we reached it there were five hundred ill in Typhus fever. An hospital was formed at Ramsgate for our reception, and the remainder going on to Deal, were with few exceptions attacked with some disease. The virulence of this disease was such, that though there were sixteen medical attendants, they were, at one time, all seized with it, except one, and when some of the others returned to duty, he also was attacked, so that not one escaped. On one day there were 30 deaths reported. While my brother, another sub, and myself, were detached in charge of the sick at Ramsgate, we were invited to dine at the mess of a Welsh Regiment, who, acting on the hospitality of those days, locked the door and kept us drinking bumper toasts till there was not a sober man in the room. Not finding any pleasure in this, I watched my opportunity, and my two neighbours, right and left, having fallen under the table, and a waiter who came in with a fresh supply of wine, having left the door open for a few minutes, I made my escape to the first bedroom I could find, and throwing myself on the bed, remained there till morning. The regiment messed at the inn.

CHAPTER II.

Walcheren Expedition—The Bay of Biscay—Ophthalmia —Arrival at Lisbon—Assassinations—Pursuit of Massena — Battle of Sabugal — Disputed Howitzer— Musketry in the Peninsula—The Bridge Marialva— Fuentes d'Onore—A *Ruse de guerre*—A Battle with Wolves—Messing and Quarters—A Slight Mistake— The Comet—Assault and Capture of Redoubt St Francisco and Ciudad Rodrigo — My Brother is Killed—Passage of the Tagus.

The 1st Battalion of the 52nd having been completed to one thousand men, it was dispatched to the Peninsula, and the 2nd Battalion, which I had joined as a lieutenant, was sent on the Walcheren expedition, which brings only two things to my recollection—the officers having to provide themselves with knapsacks, calculated to hold twenty-five pounds weight, and the fever which attacked us at its termination.

On re-embarking we all appeared in perfect health ; yet, in the course of twenty-four hours, the greater part of the battalion were in a state of delirium. I amongst the rest, found myself at Shorncliffe, having been given over, and reduced to such a state that my nearest friends would hardly know me.

The ague,which succeeds the Walcheran fever attacked me every third day, at the same hour, each fit commenced with a great depression and sense of uneasiness— the nails became blue, and a cold feel succeeded by violent shivering, which continued a considerable time, when, the animal heat returning, became equally violent in the other extreme, till a profuse perspiration gave it vent, leaving me very weak, indeed, and I barely recovered my natural strength when the next came on. The hour of its attack was at first three o'clock, but when I began to recover, it gradually got later, till I got into another day, and at last ceased. As my dinner hour was five o'clock, when I began to pass it, and I had sat down with the expectation of being able to eat it, the fit would commence, and I was obliged to rise from the table without tasting a morsel. The treatment for ague at this time was large quantities of bark, the extract of quinine not being in use.

We embarked this time on board the *Superb*, a seventy-four. The voyage was remarkable for heavy gales, in which we had our three topmasts carried away, and I saw the Bay of Biscay in all its glory ; one moment looking on the deck of a neighbouring line of battle-ship, the next looking up at her keel.

In replacing a top gallant mast, the hawser broke, when it came down by the run ; touching one of our men in the forehead ; the wound made appeared very small, not being more than an inch long and no breadth ; there was an immense flow of blood from it, but the man was dead when it appeared that the skull was split in two.

"The 1stBattalion had again landed in Portugal, and after the celebrated march of 62 miles in 26 hours, arriving in time to take the out-post duty at the close of the battle of Talavera, from whence they covered the retreat before Massena's overwhelming force, taking a prominent part in the repulse at Busaca and in the defence of the celebrated lines of Torres Vedros, by which Messena lost 5 months and was finally obliged to retreat before its defenders. We arrived in Lisbon in time to join the advance after Massena's retreating army. We joined the light division, being brigaded with our 1st Battalion, some companies of the 95th Rifles, and a battalion of Cacadores.

As we advanced after Massena's retreating army we were eye witnesses of the dreadful consequences of war. Independent of the fighting part of the business, houses in ruin, some burnt with their inhabitants in them, those that could, having fled. England may be thankful as having escaped invasion by meeting the enemy at a distance. The 2nd Battalion was not actively engaged till the combat of Sabugal, 3rd April, 1811.

It was brought on by mistake, Lord Wellington's intention being to turn the enemy's left; but the officer in temporary command of the division did not sufficiently explain the order to the Brigadiers, and our first brigade was misled by a staff officer to take the bull by the horns and attack a corps d'armie which occupied a strong position, moreover the General had carried off the cavalry which should have been ready to give us their assistance. Hearing the first brigade under Sir Sidney Beckwith engaged, our brigade returned to their support. The 1st Battalion arrived just in time to save them and capture a howitzer. It was taken by my brother's company from the enemy. The enemy made several desperate attempts to retake it from my brother, who, with two other companies of the 52nd, held their ground and the howitzer by lining a walk in its rear. We came up on the right of the 1st Battalion, which had been waging an unequal battle with a powerful adversary. We advanced in line, being received by a heavy cannonade and volleys of musketry which we returned with interest, the enemy retreating before us. I take this occasion to point out the advantage derived from the percussion caps now in use. A heavy downfall of rain occurring in the middle of our advance, the firing on both sides ceased on the instant—not a musket would go off. Notwithstanding the deficiencies we laboured under, a volley from the 52nd was a tremendous visitation. The companies under my brother's immediate orders did great execution on the French, who endeavoured to wrest the captured howitzer from them. The individual firing was singularly good. Two instances occur to me. At Fuentes d'Onore an officer's servant, riding a runaway horse, galloped through our chain of sentries, who, supposing that he was deserting to the enemy, then not many yards distant, fired at him and knocked him off the horse. Another instance was after the battle of Salamanca, when Sir Stapleton Cotton, coming in from the front, did not hear the sentriys' challange and continued to advance, on which the sentry fired and shot him through the leg. Such was not the practice of the army, as I may safely say that not one shot in a hundred told. Sir John Moore's system of raising the musket from the "Rest," instead of letting it fall from the "Present," I believe to be the cause of this surprising difference. The double sight might have some effect but I do not think it was much used, On the evening of the combat I went to my brother's quarters at Sabugal, and found him at his mess partaking of a ham cut off the howitzer so much talked about.

Having had some correspondence in the *Naval and Military Gazette* on the subject of this howitzer, relative to the mistake which occurred in the Duke's dispatch founded on Sir Sidney Beckwith's report, taking credit to his brigade for its capture, it drew forth the following remarks from Major-General W. Napier in the *Gazette* of the 28th June, 1845, which appeal having remained unanswered to the present moment, we may consider the claims of the 52nd to be acknowledged, which they were, at the time, by Captain W. C. Madden, late of the 43rd, who is now a clergyman in the Church of England :—

"1 was lying wounded in the rere at the time the combat of Sabugal was fought, and I am, of course, entirely dependent on my authorities ; but I call upon the officers of the 43rd who still live, upon those of the Riflemen, of the aitillery, of the staff, to declare whether the 43rd took the howitzer and lost it again, or 'gallantly gained and preserved it,' as the Duke of Wellington said in his dispatch. I do not mean to say that the fire of the artillery and some of the rifles did not contribute to the first gaining and then keeping of the howitzer; but I maintain, in opposition to Colonel Gurwood, as confidently as a man who was not an eye-witness can be allowed to do, the following propositions:—

1st That the howitzer was taken by the 43rd in a charge to its front.

2nd That it remained on the spot where it was taken under the fire of the 43rd until the French retreated entirely; and, consequently, that the 43rd never lost the howitzer.

3rd That the 43rd Regiment never turned during the day, though at one time two companies on the left, being overpowered with numbers, shifted to gain advantageous ground, as their great knowledge of war and their cool intrepidity dictated.

There are plenty of officers who can respond to the call I make, and some of them I feel will do so. Colonel Belson, of the artillery, General Sir A. Cameron, formerly of the Rifles, General Brown, the Dep. Adjutant-General Duffy, General J. Considine, Assistant-Inspector General Gilhurst, Colonel Patrickson, General J. Ferguson, Colonel Dazell, Sir G. Houlton, Major Hopkins, were all present at the battle in a position to know the facts. Many others have gone to their last home since my last volume was published; but if those I have mentioned come forward, and do not corroborate the Duke's dispatch, and what I have said, I have nothing more to offer; and the 43rd must bear the stigma of having, for thirty years, received and rejoiced in honour which belonged to others.

In answer to Major-General Napier's first proposition, there is no evidence given by the 43rd of their ever having taken the howitzer.

To his second proposition, the evidence to follow from Lieutenant-Colonel Gurwood and Lieutenant O'Hara will shew that what he claims for the 43rd really belongs to the 52nd.

His third proposition it is not necessary to answer. Lieutenant Gurwood says:—

"I was acting adjutant at the time, and am competent to corroborate, from my recollection, the facts stated in the dispatch, to which I was witness—viz., that the first brigade, under Colonel Beckwith, having ad-advanced from the ground on which they had formed in line for attack, drove the enemy and might have taken from them a howitzer; but the brigade was overpowered and driven back,(having lost the howitzer,)to the ground of their first formation, when they were joined by the 2nd brigade, which formed on the flank of the 43rd. The whole then advanced under the command of Colonel Beckwith, assisted by Colonel Mellish, of the H. H. G. staff of the division. The 52nd passed the enclosure and the howitzer was recovered from the enemy who endeavoured to carry it off. The left centre of the 52nd on its advance came up to the howitzer being without horses at some distance in front of the enclosure; but immediately afterwards a fresh column of the enemy, supported by cavalry, charged the two regiments which were broken. The 52nd took refuge in the enclosure, when Captain Dobbs rallied his company and others and lined that part of the wall immediately opposite the howitzer (not a hundred yards from it), the remaining part of the battalion, under Colonel Ross, defending the other side of the enclosure, and in the act of jumping the wall my horse was shot by one of the enemy's hussars that came up to, and passed the gun, and both fell inside the enclosure, the horse being killed. By the fire from this part of the wall the enemy were prevented from taking away the howitzer—thus a second time abandoned after its capture. A sharp fire was kept up on the French cavalry, which were driven back or destroyed; and the 52nd again advanced from the enclosure upon the enemy's infantry. Lieutenant O'Hara had cut away a ham which hung from the axle tree of the howitzer."

Memorandum on the affair at Sabugal by Colonel O'Hara, late 88th Regiment:—

"Castle Taylor, Ardiaham, Galway,
"22nd May, 1843.

"I must protest against the statement in Colonel W. Napier's justification (6th vol. page xiii) in reply to Colonel Gurwood's annotation in the dispatches of the Duke of Wellington. (8th vol. page 557) relative to the capture of the howitzer at the affair of Sabugal. I was Lieutenant of the 1st Battalion, 52nd Regiment, in the company commanded by the present Colonel (then Lieut. Love) both at the Bridge of Manalva and at Sabugal; and now, after a lapse of so many years, I can recollect facts, I trust quite sufficient to establish the correctness of Colonel Gurwood's statement. We (the 52nd) advanced in line across a ravine towards the enemy in a position on some high ground opposite to us. We had nearly reached the height, when I made a rush with part of Dobbs' company, and took a large-sized howitzer. A considerable body of French cavalry were posted below the height, and were, at first, unobserved by us. We retired to a stone enclosure which fortunately was very close (about a 100 yards distant.) We then with the remainder of the regiment, which had been under cover, threw a most destructive fire on the enemy, who retired with great loss and abandoned the gun. I beg briefly to add that I cut off the howitzer a ham and some spirits, which I gave to a soldier to take care of, and whose name I remember to this day."

Lord Wellington concludes his despatch in these words:—"Although the operations of this day were, by unavoidable accidents, not performed in the manner which I intended they should, I consider the action fought by the light division, by Colonel Beckwith's brigade principally, with the whole of the 2nd corps, to be one of the most glorious that British troops were ever engaged in." And in reference to the same subject Lord Wellington's letter to Marshal Beresford, dated 4th April (see despatches, new edition, vol. iv., p. 723) written previous to the despatches which states:—"The French then seeing how weak that body was that passed, attempted to drive them down to the Coa, and then oblige the 43rd to turn. They rallied again, however, and beat in the French, but were attacked by fresh troops and Cavalry, and were obliged to retire, but formed again and beat back the enemy, and to be charged and attacked again in the same manner and beat back. They formed again, moved forward upon the enemy, and established themselves on the top of the hill in an enclosure, and here they beat off the enemy· The contest was latterly entirely for the howitzer, which was taken and retaken twice, and at last remained in our hands."

From the above facts, it must appear· that the 52nd bore a more prominent part in the contest than they got credit for in the dispatch, having taken and retaken the howitzer, which the Duke states to be the principal part of the contest. The distance from the scene prevented him from distinguishing which regiment was in the enclosure.

As my expression of a ham being cut off a howitzer seems to have puzzled some of my friends, it may be well to state that artillery officers as well as infantry officers are glad to attend to their mess comforts, and if they happen to meet with a ham or any article of that nature, they would suspend it from part of the gun carriage till it could be disposed of. While speaking of mess comforts, I have to state that there were many articles which we only procure from subtlers, who found it their interest in bringing them up from the nearest sea ports, for which articles they got great prices. Tea, ale, porter, soda water, cheese, &c., &c. Speaking of soda water—which I had no taste for—many thought a great luxury. The prices were 2s. 6d. a bottle; and those who had half-crowns to spare, and were fond of it, would call for a bottle of it and drink it off in great glee. On one occasion a Portuguese officer thought that it must be something delightful, so he called for one and drank it off; but when he got the taste of it, he threw down his half-crown and ran out of the shop. In Spain tea was used as a medicine and was only sold in apothecaries' shops. Potatoes sold for 6d. a pound. Money being generally scarce we were obliged to live on our daily rations, which consisted of a pound of biscuits or a pound and a half of soft bread, with one pound of beef, —salt or fresh—or a pound of salt pork. The fresh beef was nearly all skin and bone. I seldom got sufficient to satisfy my hunger; and yet, when we got to the Pyrenees, I was in such good condition that my friends used to call me the porpoise.

In speaking of our old muskets I forgot to remark the inferior nature of the flints, which were often bad, so that after a volley nearly one-fourth part had missed fire.

On the 25th of April, 1811, Massena, having collected his army at Ciudad Rodrigo, for the relief of Almeida, made an attack on our pickquet at the bridge of Marialva on the Azava with a large force of cavalry and infantry. There was a ford a short distance below the bridge, and the company on outlying pickquet had a subdivision at each point. Both passages were important, but the ford was considered more so than the other, consequently the captain remained at the ford and the other subdivision was under the command of his lieutenant. The relieving pickquet always arrived an hour before daylight, both pickquets remaining under arms till the daylight enabled them to ascertain there was no enemy in. On the 23rd of April the company under my brother, Captain Joseph Dobbs, being the relieving one, was under arms with the old pickquet, also a company of the 52nd. my brother being in command of all who were stationed at the ford and bridge. Just as daylight appeared he heard a heavy firing at the bridge, and having ascertained that the ford was not passable in consequence of a heavy fall of rain taking place during the night, he left a corporal and three men to watch it, and dashed off with the remainder to the bridge. He arrived most opportunely, the enemy having forced the passage, and he having seen the state of affairs whilst coming over the height above the bridge, charged down on the enemy, who, supposing that he was only the advance of a large force gave way and re-crossed the bridge, on which my brother established his men amongst the rocks on our side of the bridge; keeping up such a fire that the enemy were unable to force the passage a second time. Their manner of advance was rather singular—a drummer led the company, beating what we had nicknamed "Old Trowsers;" as long as he survived they continued to advance, but so soon as he fell they immediately turned tail and ran back, when they had to go over the same process for another attack. This continued for a considerable length of time until we, the 1st and 2nd battalions of the 52nd were able to come to the relief of the picquet, when the enemy retired to their main body at Ciudad Rodrigo. It may be supposed how much my brother exposed himself, when I state that he had a shot through his cap, another through his jacket, another cut the flap of his trousers across, and another on the blade of his sabre, now in my possession.

If the enemy had succeeded in their attack on the bridge, much mischief might have been done, as all our Horse Artillery's horses were out foraging, and their cavalry would have gone into our quarters at Gallegos, before we were prepared to receive them. According to Napier's account, the attacking force consisted of two thousand infantry, and a squadron of cavalry.

The battle of Fuentes d'Onore lasted from the 5th to the 6th May, 1811. On the morning of the first days fighting the 7th division occupied some heights at the extreme right of the position, the Light Division a plain on their left, and a wood, which communicated with the division which occupied Fuentes d'Onore. The enemy attacked the 7th division in the morning, and brought five thousand cavalry to bear on our small body of cavalry immediately in front, which was obliged to retire. We were somewhat startled by Sir Sydney Beckwith, riding up, exclaiming "they're in among you, they're in among you!" and presently we saw the troop of Horse Artillery, with their guns, surrounded by the enemy, but gallantly fighting their way out. With the most perfect coolness the three battalions 1st of the 43rd and 1st and 2nd of the 52nd, formed an echelon of squares which covered the retreat of our Horse Artillery. Lord Wellington having determined on a change of position, the 7th division were ordered to retire, and we had to do the same over the plain, to the new position; this was done by alternate squares, under a heavy cannonade, the balls sometimes hopping in and out of the square. The distance was about three miles, and marching in square a most difficult operation, as if the correct line is not kept by the front and rear faces, or the sides in file marching not looked up or well covered, the square must be broken. In the evening of the second day of the battle we were ordered

into the town, and I had one of the out-lying picquets.
A few hours before daylight I heard a rolling of wheels,
but could not tell whether the enemy was retiring or
bringing up more artillery. As our sentries were on one
side of a narrow stream, and the enemy's on the other, it
was not easy for them to get off without being perceived,
but they managed it thus : when relieving sentries, they
placed a straw figure, with a French cap on its head, and
a pole like the barrel of a musket standing on its side.
Not wishing to create a false alarm, it was some time before I could ascertain the truth, but at once reported my
suspicions to head quarters, I take this opportunity of
mentioning the terms on which we were with the enemy,
when not engaged. Our side of the stream was so steep
that we could not get at the water, while theirs was
easy of access ; on making friendly signals to them, they
filled our wooden canteens for us—we throwing them
over, and they returning them filled.

In the middle of June, 1811, Marmont having crossed
the Tagus, to co-operate with Soult in the relief of the
second siege of Badajos, we also crossed the Tagus by the
Pontoon Bridge at Vilha Velha, to support the besiegers.
While occupying a bivouac behind a wooded ridge, between Campo Major and the Caya, one of those accidents
occurred which are so frequent in hot countries. The
whole surface was covered with long dry grass, and some
of the troops having lit their fires to windward, in a few
moments it took fire, and the flames quickly spread in
every direction, setting fire to the huts, and in many instances blowing up the men's pouches. The 95th suffered most.

This accident reminds me of the depopulated state of
Spain, which causes this extent of wilderness ; the inhabitants live in villages, usually about five leagues apart,
having a circle of uncultivated land around them, generally occupied by woods, which shelter large packs of
wolves. One instance of the boldness of these wolves
occurs to me, but at this distance of time, I cannot remember at which of the villages it happened. A
flock of sheep collected during the night, on the
ground used for thrashing out corn, was attacked by a
large pack of wolves ; the alarm was given, and natives

and soldiers quickly turned out, the former directing our movements. Our plan was to form a line of sharp-shooters under the brow of a hill, and then to make an arc of a circle round the cover in which the wolves had taken shelter, making the line of sharp-shooters its chord; the circle gradually closing in, the wolves passed over the heights, and received the fire of our sharp-shooters. In this way eleven of them were killed, to the great delight of the shepherds. On second thoughts, I think the village was Casellos de Flores, it was after Marmont had relieved Rodrigo, and we had been forced to retire to the Coa, being, while quartered there orderly officer of the day, it was part of my duty to visit our out-lying picquet which was stationed in a thick wood at some distance from the village, my visit was made about midnight. While passing through the wood, the wolves were howling in every direction, and when I got to the picquet I found they had let their fire get very low, but on hearing their flying sentries challenge, some of them jumped up and stirred it, when a rush of wolves escaping took place. I do not remember an instance of their attacking live men, with the exception of an orderly dragoon, who got drunk and lay on the ground in a state of helplessness, he was killed and eaten by them, with the exception of his feet, which were preserved by his boots. I have seen horses and cows with the flesh torn off their hind quarters still alive, only the bones of others remaining, and on one occasion I found the remains of a brother officer (who was hastily buried with the men's bayonets in our retreat) torn up by them, when a few month's afterwards we passed it in advance, we only ascertained it by a piece of his shirt-tail which had a mark on it, and that not his own, but a friend's who had been killed, and whose baggage was handed over to him.

The inhabitants cultivate wheat and Indian corn in a circle, extending for about a mile round each village. The wheat, when ripe, is threshed by oxen, which are fastened by a long pole, to a post which turns with them, and keeps them in their places, as they are driven round, treading out the corn. Their ploughs are wooden ones, and barely scrape the ground; their bullock cars are equally rough, and as they never grease their axles they

make a disagreeable creaking noise. The bullocks are
harnessed to their work by a heavy piece of wood laid on
their necks and lashed to their horns, by which the poor
animals suffer dreadfully, particularly in hot weather.
Their sheep, oxen, and pigs are under 'charge of herds,
who keep dogs to assist in watching them in the uncultivated waste land. Pigs are in the best condition when
the acorns are ripe; they are driven into woods, and
brought home at night. It is an amusing sight to see
them dismissed in the evening at the entrance of the village, every one running to its own home. They make a
rush like a charge of cavalry, and if the passage is narrow,
it is rather dangerous to meet them. The houses in the
Spanish villages consist of a kitchen, in which all the
family sit, and several sleeping apartments. The kitchen
is the only room which contains a chimney; the window's
have no sashes, and are closed by wooden shutters. The
roofs are covered with tiles. These houses are very plea-
sant in summer, but most uncomfortable in winter.
When billetted on them in this season, (as it would not
do for an officer to sit in the kitchen) we had to adopt
some means of making the rooms we occupied more comfortable. We used to run up a wall at one of the corners,
leaving room for a fire at the bottom, and breaking a hole
out of the top of the chimney; this was a great annoyance to the landlords, and as the chimneys generally
smoked, was not particularly comfortable for his tenants;
the following scene occurred in consequence:—Captain
Currie, of the 52nd, was sitting over his fire, which
smoked very much; the landlord perceiving this, came in
and sat down, watching the captain, who being a very
patient man, sat very quietly without shewing his annoyance. The landlord on this grew wild, and jumping up,
exclaimed, "If you can stand fire as well as you stand
smoke, you are one of the best soldiers in His Britannic
Majesty's army." It must be remembered that wood is
the fuel used, and that it is laid on the ground. In the
better class of houses, charcoal is used in a round brass
pan, which fits into a wooden frame, on which seats can
be placed. There are some parts of the country where
there is no wood, and the inhabitants are obliged to use
straw. We found this a great hardship when we had to

bivouac, having no shelter from the sun by day, nor from the heavy dew by night, except our blankets, until there were four tents served out to each company, one for the officers, and three for the men. Our manner of cooking was adapted to our circumstances; one servant went for wood, another for water, and the third, or one of ourselves, prepared what we had to cook. By this division of labour the work was soon accomplished. Short as it was, however, I have been disturbed in it by the enemy's movements, and on one occasion had to throw out the soup, and pack up the meat three times before it was dressed; as to the last water, it could not be called soup.

Being unable to procure cow's milk, and goat's milk being very scarce, we found it a great comfort to have our own goats. We had several to each company, and they became so tame, that we found them very troublesome; they would occupy our beds, and follow us about when we did not want them. The officers of each company messed together, and had a boy to drive the goats. While on the subject of mess matters, I may mention an accident which gave me some annoyance, but which was rather an amusement to my comrades. We were engaged in preparing a dish which required pepper, and had got some red-pepper-pods for the purpose of seasoning it. Having taken one in my hand, I happened to touch my eyes and lips with my fingers, when both were set smarting in a way that drove me wild.

Our Commissariat, although greatly improved by Lord Wellington's regulations, was frequently unable to meet our necessities from want of money, and means of transport. We were frequently days without bread or salt; and the draught bullocks likely to die, were killed and served out for rations. Our pay being in arrears, we had no money to purchase what we might otherwise have procured from the natives.

It may be interresting to show the manner in which we got under arms. The old plan was by bugle calls by day, and an alarm by night in the same way; but now the most perfect silence was preserved. The commander of the division had an orderly from each brigade, who carried the order to the Brigadier, who again had an orderly from each regiment, and the regimental commander had an orderly from each company; the sergeants were obliged to get the roll of the company by heart, so that when called out at night they did not require a light for the purpose. Although these matters may appear trifling, yet they conduced greatly to the efficiency of the Light Division, of whom the Duke of Wellington was heard to say, that he gave them an order overnight, for a dangerous service, and on the following morning the work was done, and the division on parade, as if nothing had happened. Another cause of efficiency was Crawford's system of not drinking on the march, which was observed by all the old soldiers, and prevented the falling out of the ranks, which may generally be observed in younger ones.

Breaking up from the Caya on the 21st July, we recrossed the Tagus in the beginning of August. In September the Light Division was posted on the Vadilla, and were employed making fascines and gabions for the siege of Rodrigo. Shortly after this the famous comet made its appearance; it was very fine, but I consider that of 1858 finer.

The Light Division being engaged in the distant investment of Ciudad Rodrigo, were cut off from the rest of the army by the advance of the enemy for its relief. The latter having effected their purpose, crossed the Aguada on the 25th of September, and attacked our forces at Elbedon, by which movement they got into our rear, and our division had to work round their flank to rejoin the main body. The baggage had to make a still greater detour through the woods, and under the mountain. Our baggage guard consisted of the two Batmen belonging to each company, with some others belonging to the staff, an officer of each battalion having the command. The tail of each company's mules being tied to its follower were led by one of the batmen, the other being left free to act as circumstances might require. Having the baggage guard on this occasion, while passing through the wood after nightfall, I met two officers wearing cocked hats and blue frock coats, and supposing them to be Frenchmen, I called for one or two of the batmen, and seized the bridle of one of the horses. I found, however, that my prisoners were Major O'Kelly of the 11th and another officer who were out reconnoitering. About two years after this, I was crossing the Crown mountain, on my way to join the 5th Caçadores at the siege of St. Sebastian, and was leading my horse down the mountain, when I was overtaken by a field officer, who was also leading his horse. We entered into conversation, and after some time he said, " I have heard your voice before ;" I replied that I had no recollection of having ever met him. He said, " Do you remember taking me prisoner in a wood near the Vadilla, and calling out to your men, ' Come here one or two of you' ?" Major O'Kelly was perfect in all the languages spoken in the Peninsula, and was particularly adapted to the service in which I first met him. No one could guess to what nation he belonged.

After my encounter with Major O'Kelly we came to an extensive bivouac, and going forward with a file of men to reconnoitre, to our surprise we were allowed to approach close to one of their fires without challenge, when we heard the greatest confusion of language spoken. These were men in charge of Commissariat and Ordnance stores, &c.; they were composed of Portuguese, Spaniards, Germans, and English, who were in the same predicament as ourselves. The next day we rejoined the army at Fuente Guinalda, having found that the enemy had a few hours previously been on the ground we had marched over.

Lord Wellington having retired to Nava de Vere during the night our chaplain remaining after the troops, was taken by the enemy, and after a few days was sent back as a non-combatant, but such articles of his baggage as were found useful retained.

This leads me to remark, that during the whole period of my foreign service in the Peninsula, Sweden or Walcheren, the regiment was never once assembled for Divine Service, nor could the Lord's day be distinguished from week days.

Some time after Massena's retreat, an officer, son of an eminent dentist in Dublin, being left in the rear, in charge of sick and wounded, was in the habit of visiting them for the purpose of reading the scriptures, or speaking to them on religious subjects; his conduct was immediately reported to Lord Wellington, with a request that he might be reprimanded. His lordship's reply was that he did not see how he could interfere, so long as he did not neglect his own duty. At this time it was supposed that a christian must necessarily be a milksop and a coward, and was looked upon with great contempt.

As soon as the French retired the troops were quartered in theVilages, on the left bank of the Aguada, close to Rodrigo, we were quartered in Elbedon.

In crossing the Aguada to take our tour of duty in the siege of Cuidad Rodrigo, we had to ford it, the water being up to our hips; and as there was a heavy hoar frost during the whole period of the siege, and we lay on the bare ground for six hours during the night, with only a single blanket to cover us, we were sufficiently cooled; our blankets after the night were stiff enough to stand upright. About this time, I had risen to the head of the 2nd Battalion Lieutenants, and was transferred to the 1st Battalion as Junior Lieutenant. I was attached to my brother's Company.

On the 8th of January, 1812, the first night of the siege, the company was engaged with Sir John Colbourn in storming the redoubt of St. Francisco; his orders were so plain that no man could mistake his post. The redoubt was attacked on all sides at once, and I believe every man of its garrison could be accounted for as killed or prisoner. As soon as it was carried I was telling off the company on the glacis, when Sir John (now Lord Seaton) expressed his satisfaction at my conduct to my brother. After having carried it we advanced to a water-course just under the walls, to prevent a sortie by the enemy on our working party, who were breaking ground on a line with the redoubt we had taken; the French had their breaching batteries on this spot when they were taking it from the Spaniards.

As soon as the enemy ascertained that the redoubt was in our possession, they opened a tremendous fire of shot and shell on it, all of which passed over our heads. We lay there till daylight, when we were obliged to retire to a more covered position.

The duty for the twenty-four hours was, six hours trenches and six hours out of them, alternately. The trench duty was six hours working and six hours covering, and then we had our hip-bath in the Aguada on our return to quarters at Elbedon.

On the last day of the siege, the 19th January, 1812, the four divisions being collected for the assault, my brother, being the second senior captain with the Regiment, claimed the right of leading the column; the Regimental order being, the senior Captain's Company on the right, the next in order on the left of the Battalion, and so on, and the order of attack being "Left in front;" this placed him by the side of General Vandeleur and Lieutenant Colonel Colbourn. On their reaching the head of the breach there was a volley from their flank which the General and Lieutenant Colonel received in their shoulders and which cost my poor brother his life.

We and the 43rd moved up the breach in sections of threes, my post was in rear of the company. The orders were to wheel to the left after mounting the breach, and so to compass the ramparts on its right, while the 43rd did the same to its left, which brought them into the rear of the defenders of the large breach.

When I got to the head of the breach, I found Colonel Colbourn, although wounded, directing the head of the column, with which I passed on, not knowing my poor brother's fate till morning.

After the siege of Rodrigo, we were sent into winter quarters, and everything appeared to be at a stand-still. Lord Wellington's hounds were sent out to the front, as if he was satisfied with what had been done, and only thought of his amusement. The French generals who had failed in the relief of Rodrigo, also took up their winter quarters, not suspecting any further movement on our part. But Lord Wellington was hard at work getting up his siege train by the Tagus, and suddenly moved across that river by the bridge of Vilha Velha. The siege train had been lying at Elvas, where the necessary fascines and gabions had also been prepared.

About this time I cut my "wisdom teeth," the torture was very great, and my bed very hard, the bedstead being a door, and the bedding a cloak and blanket, and the pillow my servant's knapsack.

CHAPTER III.

Siege of Badajos—Captain Jones—Crossing the Tormes —Battle of Salamanca—Advance on and capture of Madrid—Ordered to Gatafe—Bull Fight--Retreat from Burgos and Salamanca—Hardships of the Retreat— Our Arrival at Rodrigo.

Arriving at Badajos on the 17th of March, 1812, we broke ground after nightfall. A heavy fall of rain, high wind, and the nature of the ground, which was a deep bed of clay, prevented the enemy in Fort Pecurina from hearing or seeing us, although only about one hundred and sixty yards distant. At Ciudad Rodrigo, the surface being gravel, every blow of the pickaxe was heard, and the sparks of fire from the gravel were seen; at Badajos, on the other hand, the constant rain caused the trenches to become beds of mud.

The enemy's shell's at Rodrigo were more destructive than at Badajos, the surface being hard, the shells did not sink into the ground, consequently fell in all directions, while at Badajos, they sank into the clay, and you could lie quite close to them without danger, the splinters flying upwards. To persons who have not read on the subject it may be well to state that, in every battery there is a person on the look out, who calls out at every discharge from the enemy, ball or shell, as it may be; when the former each person covers himself behind the parapet; if the latter, it was watched as it took its course through the air till it fell; if close, you fell flat on the ground, till it exploded; if at a distance, you had to take your chance.

We had, however, the advantage of being within half an hour's march of our tents; but even the tents in heavy rain were anything but comfortable, and besides, were within range of the enemy's guns. Our camp was to the left of the inundation, which ran between our trenches and the town.

In the storming of Fort Pecurina, which was done by the 3rd Division, and some of our Division, Captain

Madden of the 52nd, (who had been out shooting, and had a shooting jacket on) followed the stormers into the fort. Here he became exposed to the fire of both sides, as neither could tell what he was; however he escaped unhurt. He was under the impression that he was invulnerable, but unfortunately for his theory, he was killed in storming the breaches on the last night of the siege. His brother of the 43rd was supposed to be mortally wounded in the same attack. On this occasion, for the first time, I heard a complaint of the want of the Sacred Scriptures; there was not a copy to be found amongst us. I am happy to say, that in this respect the state of things is altered.

On the opening of one of our first counter-batteries, I happened to be in the covering party, and occupied a trench in its front, running parallel to the battery; the enemy opened a tremendous fire on it, and in a short time dismounted several guns and disabled others. On this a message came to us requesting that we would endeavour to stop the enemy's fire. Accordingly we opened fire on their embrasures, and the effect of the fire was such, that in about twenty minutes they had to stop them with gabions. Some of the shots struck the sides and glanced right and left—others went right through the centre, so that the gunners could not stand to their guns. I do not remember our distance from the walls, but the trench ran along the front of the batteries, about fifty yards nearer to the walls.

On the 6th April the fourth and light divisions got under arms at sunset, and as soon as it was dark moved along the left bank of the stream, and inundation to the attack of the three breaches. The left hand one was in the face of the Bastion and impracticable, the centre and large one, in the curtain, and right hand one in the flank of the next bastion. The centre and right hand ones were perpendicular; Philipon, having had the rubbish cleared away from the breaches every night, which could not be prevented, as our breaching batteries from their distance could not be brought to bear on the wall lower than the glacis. The head of the breaches after our batteries had stopped for the night were enclosed by a chevaux de frize of sword blades, fastened by chains and bags of old iron, barrels full of nails, and boards with nails sticking out of them. The former were prepared to roll down on the stormers, and the latter to lie flat on the breach. Shells were ranged along the parapet and howitzers, and morters placed so as to throw fire balls into the ditch. The head of each breach and the connecting parapet were lined with men, those at the breaches having fresh loaded muskets handed to them in exchange for those discharged, beside a ball cartrage, each musket contained a round piece of wood with eight slugs stuck into eight holes, which on the discharge were separated like a discharge of grape, supposing the breaches carried. A deep ditch, defended by a breast-work, would have to be carried; the ditch appeared to me to be 24 feet deep, and in front of the curtain was an unfinished ravelin. The inundation flooded the ditch up to the ravelin, and opposite the left hand breach its depth exceeded six or seven feet. Such was the defence we had to encounter, our descent into the ditch was effected by ladders, from ignorance of the depth of water opposite the left hand breach, several of the ladders were placed in it, and the consequence was, a number of men were drowned in it. Our orders were, not to fire a shot, and, if I recollect right, the men were not permitted to load. To obviate this defenceless state a number of rifle men were placed on the glacis to fire over our heads till we could reach the breaches. As I was attached to one of the rear companies, I had an opportunity of seeing the commencement of the assault and defence. As soon as the head of the column was discovered, the enemy opened on us with shot, shell, and musketry, first having ascertained our whereabouts by fire balls; but when the ditch became crowded with men, the shells on the parapet were lighted and thrown over, fire balls were thrown into the ditch, so that every man could be seen and exposed to a murderous fire of musketry. The ladder, I descended was at the edge of the inundation, and I got into about a foot of water at first. I turned to my right, and finding the water get deeper, I retraced my steps, and came to the unfinished ravelin (which I fancied to be one of the breaches), and shouting to the men to come on, found our mistake. As no impression could be made on the breach, every man mounting being swept down, and the whole ditch crowded with men, dead and alive, we remained under fire for two hours, till Lord Wellington sent word that the Castle was taken, and ordered the men out of the ditch to reform, which was done in a gravel-pit close to the glacis; and as numbers had gone off with wounded men to the hospital tents, I was sent to bring them back. Having done so, at day light, we were marching to the breaches, and having succeeded in removing, the obstruction made good our entrance. The scene in the ditch was dreadful, and as we mounted the breach we met some prisoners coming out. One of them, an officer, who, looking on the dead bodies lying before him, smiled at them, which so enraged one of our men, that he knocked him down.

The siege of Badajos cost us more men and officers than any other siege or action we were engaged in. There were seven captains killed or wounded in the ditch— three of them killed, and one died of his wound; twenty-two officers, and seventy non-commissioned officers and men. There were only eight officers fit for duty on the 7th April, the day after the assault.

Captain Jones, our senior captain, was one of the killed; he was a very brave and gallant officer. We had been chatting together a few hours before the storming. He was a Welshman, and had a gruff way of speaking, in addition to his native accent. Speaking of the assault, he said, " I'll be a man or a mouse to-night." He commanded our hundred stormers at Rodrigo; and a short time after it was in our possession, finding a number of the soldiers in a church sitting round a fire which they had lit on the pavement (having previously ascertained that it was used as a magazine, and that a great number of barrels of powder were piled at the end of it), he immediately turned the men out, and with his own hands carefully carried out each brand, and had the door secured. At the battle of Busaco, the enemy advancing in a column of grand divisions, their right hand company came in contact with our right hand flank company, the regiment being in line; the company was commanded by Captain Jones, the captains met hand to hand, and the Frenchman was killed in the encounter.

Those who lay great stress on presentiments, will find something to unsettle this idea in the feelings of the three captains killed at Badajos. Captain Madden thought himself invulnerable, Captain Jones looked on it as a doubtful case, and Captain Poole expressed himself as going to certain death.

When we got into Badajos, through the breaches, the enemy having abandoned them, when the Castle was taken by the third divisions, it was found impossible to keep the men together, and a scene of plunder and drunkenness took place of the worst character, and it was found necessary for some time to let it take its course. I had a narrow escape from some drunken men who were following a bull through a street, as I was coming from the other end, they fired a folley at it which passed me in all directions.

Having returned to camp, the men began gradually to return, laden with plunder—some dressed as monks, others in female dresses, some as Frenchmen officers. All we could do was to keep them from going back, and they gradually returned to duty.

On the 8th April I was ordered on command, with all the wounded that could be moved, to Elvas. On going to take charge I found the surgeon still busily employed in cutting off legs and arms, of which there was an immense heap close to the hospital tents. Surgeon Maling was a man of first class abilities in his profession; he was rather rough in his manner, but very prompt to act. I found him on this occasion with his coat off, his sleeves tucked up, his patient stretched upon a table, and the knife in his hand, and after a sweeping cut round the limb, he would take the knife between his teeth that he might have his hands free to tie up the arteries. When a case of emergency arose he would throw off his coat and tuck up his sleeves, which action gave him among the men the nickname of " Short Sleeves.. One look was sufficient to satisfy him when a man was shamming. I am proud to say we had few of this class. My orders were to deliver my charge at the hospital, formed at Elvas, and to return at once to the regiment, from which I could not be spared. Mules and bullock cars were provided for the wounded ; many of them had their arms amputated on the night of the storm, and others with slight wounds preferred walking to riding, the shaking causing them greater pain than moving on their feet. I arrived late in the day, placed my charge in safety, and returned to my regiment, having escaped an attack from some brigands whom I passed in the dark. They gave me a few shots to hasten my return. I arrived before daylight, and found the battalion under orders to cross the Tagus at Vilha Velha, to put a stop to the advance of Marmont, who had entered Portugal, and was threatening Almeida and Ciudad Rodrigo, and was doing all the mischief he could in our rear. Soult was only a few marches from Badajos when it was taken ; in a day or two more we should have had to raise the siege.

Marmont retiring on our approach we enjoyed about two months' rest, during which time most of our wounded re-joined, and in June we began our advance on Salamanca.

From this period we found a great change for the better in the Spaniards. We were received with shouts of long life to the English, and in the large cities the windows were crowded with beautiful females waving their handkerchiefs as we passed through the streets at our entrance. They were allowed to walk only as Spanish women can walk, on their pradoes, in full dress, being a great compliment to us and an indulgence to them.

On the 17th of June we passed the Tormes, leaving Salamanca in our rear, and having the 6th Division engaged in the seige of the French forts. On the 20th Marmont advanced to our front with four divisions and a brigade of *cavalry*, and on the 22nd he received three more divisions and another brigade of cavalry. These additions enabled him to make an attack on our right, which was repulsed by General Graham with the 7th division, on which the French retired about six miles. On the 27th, the forts had fallen, Marmont retreated behind the Douro followed by the British ; but having obtained large reinforcements, he was again enabled to commence offensive operations, constantly out-flanking us. On the 17th July we were marching in parallel columns, at about a stone's throw from one another—it was a beautiful sight and continued for ten miles. The question was, who should arrive first at the river Guarena. We accomplished our object; when the enemy finding we had slipped through their fingers, opened a heavy cannonade on our column. The weather being very sultry, and our men suffering from thirst, they contrived to slack it by dipping their hands in the water as they marched through it. We soon got into communication with the rest of the army, who were in a strong position on the banks of the river. On the 21st of July, the enemy having crossed the Tormes between Alba de Tormes and Huerta, we also crossed it lower down. The night was dark, and a tremendous storm of thunder, lightning and rain was raging while we passed down the bank of the river to the ground marked out for our encampment. We had been allowed four bell-tents to each company—one for the officers and three for the men; there was great difficulty in pitching them, and when pitched they afforded very poor shelter, and were blown down once or twice in the night. In the middle of the night some of the cavalry horses broke from their picquets and galloped through the camp, so that it was supposed that the enemy were amongst us; and it was some time before it could be ascertained what was the matter.

The British position on the 22nd was two sides of a right angled triangle. We occupied the centre, and had an opportunity of seeing all the movements going forward, up to the advance of the 3rd Division and Bradford's Portuguese Brigade—to the latter of which I was afterwards attached as a captain in the 5th Cacadores. About five o'clock in the evening I was looking at the French troops who were moving towards the right, with the intention of cutting off the communication with Ciudad Rodrigo, when I exclaimed to some brother officers, with whom I was conversing, "O! that we had a Division at that hill." While I was speaking the 3rd Division made its appearance from behind it, and the rout of the French army was the consequence. We were ordered to advance, and we chased the enemy till darkness prevented further pursuit. On the 23rd the enemy formed a rear-guard from the confusion which prevailed the night before; and the heavy German

Cavalry, supported by the light division, commenced an active pursuit. The Germans charged the enemy's squares and broke them, on which the latter threw down their arms (which lay as if regularly grounded) and fled over the plain pursued by the Germans to whom they surrendered as they came up. It was amusing to see a single horseman riding back to us with a crowd of Frenchmen around him. It must, however, be remembered that being without arms they were exposed to a worse enemy—the Partidas—and were therefore glad to have British protection.

The effect of the battle of Barossa, won by Graham, the surprise of Almaras, by Hill, the capture of Ciudad Rodrigo, Badajos and the forts of Salamanca, and of the battle of Salamanca, were the relief of Cadiz, and the junction of Graham's army with that of Lord Wellington, while Hill was advancing closer. The French army had been obliged to retire from the advanced positions and formed a more contracted one around the British—having Clauzel in command of the right, Joseph of the centre, and Soult of the left. The battle of Salamanca had paralysed them, and Lord Wellington advanced to Burgos on the left, and Madrid in the centre. The Light Division with Lord Wellington's main body, and Hill on the right, drove Joseph and his army before them to Madrid ; which they were obliged to evacuate in the greatest confusion, leaving behind them in the retire, a garrison of two thousand men, and enormous stores—one hundred and eighty pieces of artillery, twenty thousand stand of arms, &c., all of which were surrendered without a shot. As we crossed the Guaderama we came upon the famous palace of the Escurial, which many of us took the opportunity of visiting. It was built by a Spanish king, in honour of St. Laurence, said to be martyred by being broiled on a gridiron ; the outer building is a square, representing the frame of a gridiron, while there are a number of smaller buildings representing the bars of it. The building contains a residence for the Royal family, also accommodation for a number of monks ! having a fine place of worship, Cloisters, &c. The burial place of the Royal family is also here, its entrance is by a beautiful staircase, lined with marble, which leads to the splendid marble apartment I think eight sided, having marble coffins ranged in inches, one above the other, each containing a crowned head.

There are other apartments in this part of the building, one containing the members of the Royal family, in wooden berths like those of the cabin of a packet. The bodies are embalmed, and baked in two ovens prepared, one for the men and the other for the women. Their coffins had been opened by the French, and left exposed to view, in their full dress—I took two silk buttons off John of Austrias dress, what became of them, I cannot tell.

We arrived at Madrid on the 12th of August, 1812, and after the surrender of the Retiro our Brigade was sent to the advanced post of Gatafe, where we remained till obliged to retreat after the failure at Burgos. While we remained at Gatafe we had an invitation from the Spaniards to witness one of their bull-fights at Madrid, and another from Lord Wellington to a splendid ball and supper, to which all went who could be spared. It was given in Joseph's palace, and we had some of Joseph's wine which was of the first quality.

The bull-fight, I will endeavour concisely to describe, although I fear it may prove uninteresting to most of my readers. It is held in an immense uncovered circus, surrounded by a strong barricade about four feet high, having a passage about six feet broad between it and the front seats prepared for the spectators ; these are tire above tire being divided into boxes, and having a splendid one provided for Royalty, or the authority who presides. On one side of the circus there is an entrance by folding doors, and at the other an entrance from the apartment from which the bull is to enter having also folding doors. The scene commences with all the spearmen entering the circus through the door opposite the Royal box, and having saluted the person or persons representing Royalty, they retire with the exception of two ; these place themselves in front of the door by which the bull is to enter, which being thrown open after a flourish of trumpets, he generally enters with a bound, having a number of pigeons which had been confined with him fluttering about his head. On seeing the vast concourse

of people, he generally stops and looks about with surprise, till beholding the two horsemen motionless before
him, he gives a bellow, and begins tearing the ground
with his feet, and taking his aim, lowers his head! and
charges one of the horsemen whose spear is lowered to
meet him, and when rightly directed catches him in the
shoulder and turns him off. The spear can only enter
about an inch into the animal, having a ball at the end
which prevents its doing more. Should the horseman
miss his aim the bull gets under the horse, tossing him
and the rider over, and generally leaving the poor horse,
when he rises, with his bowels hanging out, the man is
seldom hurt. Immediately on the accident taking place,
a number of men with small flags in their hands jump
over the barricade into the circus, flirting them into the
bull's face till he is drawn off from the horse and man,
and when he runs at them they jump back into the passage between the barricade and audience. When the
bulls are very active they sometimes jump over the barricade too, on which the flagmen jump into the circus, and
the bull proceeds on till he comes to a door left open for
the purpose and again enters the circus, the door is then
shut and the flagmen jump into the passage. After
several encounters with the horsemen he gets tired of attacking them, when the flagmen proceed to tease them
first with the flags, only jumping over the barricade
whenever he makes a rush on them that they cannot
otherwise escape. When the bull is two quiet they have
small darts with lighted fireworks attached, which being
stuck into the animal give him great annoyance; some
of the most active flagmen jump across his head and
strike a couple of these darts into his neck behind his
horns. After this has continued some time they retire,
and the matadore or killer enters the circus, armed with
a long straight sword, sharp at both sides and tapering to
a point in his right hand, and one of the flags in his left,
he advances to the bull, whose experience and fatigue has
made more cautious, and standing before him waits his
attack, which at last takes place; having taken his aim
first, the bull lowers his head and shuts his eyes, and
makes a rush at the man, which he dexterously avoids by
moving to the left, and receiving it on the flag in his left

hand, which is held across his body, and with the right enters the sword above the shoulder, on which the bull empales himself and falls dead.

The entrance door is then thrown open, and two mules gaily caparisoned are driven in and fastened to the bull, dragging him out of the circus, which is then raked over and made ready for another bull-fight. In this manner sixteen bulls met their death, the seventeenth was beaten with dogs, and then killed by the matadore; it was the middle one of the sixteen beaten by men, eight preceded it and eight succeeded it; a number of dogs, after several being killed succeeded in pinning it, so that it could not move, when the matadore killed it by running his sword through the body in different parts.

The first horse was gored with his bowels hanging out. The Spanish audience, particularly the women, called on the spearman to mount again. This struck us as an extra act of cruelty, and we cried out against it, and made such a row as prevented his doing so, and the horse was removed and a fresh one brought in.

On the 23rd of August we left Gatafe on our way to Salmanca. A little way on the Madrid side of the Guaderama Pass, and not far from the Escurial, we were halted with our arms piled, when a wild boar was started, which was the occasion of a singular state of confusion. A general attack was made on him, some of the men throwing themselves on his back, others trying to get a blow at him as he ran among the piled arms; at last a butcher got a blow at him with his axe, and struck him on the head, when he was soon dispatched.

Having joined the troops retreating from Burgos, we took the rear-guard, and commenced our retreat from Salmanca on the 15th of November, 1812.

Soult having turned our flank, we were engaged in covering the retreat of the army on the 15th and 16th of November. The forests we were passing through were occupied by numerous herds of pigs, feeding on the acorns which fell from the trees; the divisions that preceded us pursued and killed numbers of them, creating an alarm by their firing. Our men were free from blame in this matter—however they might be inclined, they were too near the enemy to attempt it. I must observe that we were here suffering from want of rations, as by a mistake the ration bullocks had been sent to the rear with the baggage.

On the 17th the division bivouacked on a hill sloping to the front, with a valley behind. While the men were folding their blankets I happened to go to the rear, and on looking into the valley saw several French dragoons riding at their leisure. I lost no time in giving the alarm; it appeared that our cavalry pickets had retired without giving us notice. During this day the enemy's cavalry were in our rear and upon our flank, and we were obliged to march in column at quarter distance, and frequently to form squares. On one occasion, General Vandeleur and his staff had to take shelter in ours. Gen. Vandeleur had never served with infantry till he got command of our brigade. And as some of the distance had been lost by some of the rear companies, when the sections wheeled up to form square, there was a gap in the square which I was putting to rights by making all the men close in by side step, this appeared to him confusion; and he returned me thanks for my exertion, which was nothing out of the common. During this day's retreat, General Paget and part of our baggage were carried off from between the head of our division and the rear of his own, the 1st division; and finally, under the fire of thirty pieces of cannon, we crossed the Huibra, and occupied an oak wood in defence of the lower fords.

In passing along the banks of this river, the French threw a number of shells amongst us, but they did us no injury, from the bank being covered with a bed of soft mud, in which they sank so deep, that in the explosion, nothing but clay was thrown up. When we got into a position, the French attempted to take it from us, in repulsing which Captain Dawson of the 52nd was killed. Being short of rations we were glad to pick up the acorns knocked down by the French bullets. During the night we had to bivouac on the ground which was flooded to the depth of several inches. We contrived to collect some stones into a heap, which enabled us to light a fire, but we actually lay in the water some inches deep during the night. On the 18th we continued the retreat, knee-deep in water. I have had many severe marches, but this was

the worst I ever experienced. When we got to a rising
ground, on which we were to bivouac, I fell completely
exhausted. We arrived the next day at Rodrigo, and
took up our winter quarters, after experiencing the heavy
rains of spring at Badajos, and the heavy rains of autumn
in the retreat. Few in this country can have any idea of
their violence.

CHAPTER IV.

Advance on Vittoria—Fall of Burgos—Affair of San
Milan—Battle of Vittoria—Pursuit of Clausel—Line
of March—A Sagacious Horse—Battle of the Pyrenees
—Assault and attempted relief of St. Sebastian—Crossing of the Bidassoa.

Having rested for five months, we started from Fuentes
Guinalda on the 20th of May, 1813, to lead the advance
of the main body of Lord Wellington's army. General
Hill commanded the right wing, and General Graham the
left. We passed the Douro on the 3rd of June, at the
bridge of Toro, which had to be repaired for our passage,
the French having previously blown it up. Lieutenant
Pringle of the Engineers effected this by dropping ladders
on each side, and laying planks from one to the other, a
little above the water.

On the 12th of June, the Light Division, led by Grant's
Hussars and Ponsonby's Dragoons, turned the French
right, while the remainder of the troops attacked them in
front, and turned their left, forcing them to retire. In
retreating they blew up the Castle of Burgos, and by
some mismanagement destroyed more than three hundred
of their own men. Thus was effected without a shot on
our part, that which had cost us so dearly to attempt in
the last year's campaign. On the 13th we passed the
Ebro.

Previous to our reaching the valley of the Ebro we had
been marching over a plain to which there appeared to
be no end, having no vegitation, when suddenly we found
ourselves looking down into a beautiful valley, thickly
planted with fruit trees, &c., and the river running in the
centre; here we obtained many luxuries, of which we had
been long deprived so far as our funds would allow, being

several months pay in arrears; part of this advance we were obliged to cook with choped straw, having no other fuel.

On the 18th of June we came across a French Brigade halting on the bank of a rivulet, waiting for a second brigade and their baggage. Both brigades were routed: the men threw away their knapsacks and made their escape, with the loss of at least three hundred prisoners and all their baggage. They then crossed the Zadora, where all the French armies were collecting to stop our progress.

On 21st the Light Division advanced to the neighbourhood of the Zadora, and were halted on a height from which we had a full view of General Hill's movements on the extreme right, while Graham was turning the extreme left. General Hill attacked and drove the enemy from the heights occupied by their left wing. It was gallantly done, and was what Wellington was waiting for; to push forward the centre under his own immediate direction.

We were ordered to advance to the attack and under a heavy cannonade crossed one of the bridges over the Zadora. The seventh division having crossed another bridge on our left, our brigade was sent to re-enforce them. We found them heavily raked by a French battery on their right. On this the 52nd, under Colonel Gibbs, advanced in column along the front of the height on which the guns were, and wheeling into line it was found necessary by an echelon movement to take up a new alignment. This was done with the same precision as it would be on a field-day, and a beautiful line was formed, the enemy's balls knocking a file out of it at every discharge; the serjeants in rear calling out "Who got that?" and entering the names on their list, of casualties. The regiment then charged up the hill receiving a volley of grape without much loss, and driving the enemy before them over the plain on which Vittoria was situated. On this occasion our column of advance was at first in subdivisions, we were left in front, and I had the command of one when a ball from the French battery passed over my head, and struck the third man on my left on the shoulder, taking his head off without doing more injury. He had only just joined us from home, and had said to his comrade the night before that he thought he would be killed in the expected battle. The cavalry presently came up, passed us, and took the pursuit. On reaching the city we found its neighbourhood covered with guns, baggage, stores of all descriptions, waggons full of money, carriages and conveyances of all kinds, with the immense concourse of Joseph's court. Of the siege trains and field batteries only two guns were carried off, one of which was disabled by a shot from our Horse Artillery, and taken on the 24th, as we continued the pursuit.

While passing through the centre of this immense body not a man was allowed to fall out, so that not an article was touched by us ; stragglers and camp-followers were able to load themselves with it at their leisure. Indeed it may be said that the hard-working men of the Peninsular, generally speaking, got more kicks than half-pence. We were eighteen hours under arms on the 31st, having started at day-break, and followed the retreating enemy till darkness stopped their pursuit.

Clausel having on the 22nd of June (on his approach to Vittoria with fourteen thousand men) found the state of affairs, retired to Logrona, where he halted until the evening of the 25th, when Lord Wellington having got information of his movements sent the 5th and 6th divisions after him, and proceeded with the 3rd, 4th and 7th, and the Light Division, with two brigades of Light Cavalry to intercept him, as he was making his way into France by Olite and Tafalla. We accomplished this by a long and weary night's march over the mountains, which lay between Pampeluna and these towns. Our division, after driving the only remaining gun which escaped from Vittoria into Pampeluna, left General Hill, with the 2nd division, to form its siege, and proceeded on the night march alluded to above. The part of the mountain we passed over would only admit of an advance in single file. Our general line of march was in sections of three's, which information was particularly suited to the Penin-sular roads. The officer commanding the company rode at its head, the senior sub in the rear, the second with the captain in the front, and third sub with the first in the rear. For this purpose the companies were told off into three's, but instead of the old plans, the sections wheeled on its flank, and the command three's right, left, or front, was particularly adapted to the service, as well as the nature of the country. The state of the weather was similar to that of the night before the battle of Salmanca—there being torrents of rain, attended by tremendous peals of thunder and vivid flashes of lightning.

Having crossed the mountain, we were halted for the rear to close up, and I lay down with my horse's bridle over my arm. He had been a French troop horse, was taken at the battle of Fuentes d'Onore, and purchased from his captor by my brother. He would follow me about like a dog, and on this occasion, in the " war of elements," remained by me while I slept. He would hold up his mouth to be kissed, and would stretch out his legs when ordered to do so, till his belly was nearly touching the ground, so that the rider could throw his leg over him without the use of the stirrup. Poor fellow, after seeing much hard service with his old masters, the French, and a good deal with ourselves, he lost his life in consequence of our being obliged to feed our horses on chopped furze ; some of the spikes stuck in his tongue and could not be extracted, in consequence of which he was unable to eat and died from starvation.

During our passage over the mountain, Graham had driven Foy over the Bidasso, and invested St. Sebastian, while Hill had driven Joseph and the remnant of his force into France, leaving the whole frontier of Spain, from the mouth of the Bidasso to Roncesvalles, in our possession, with the exception of the two besieged cities.

At this time Soult superseded Joseph, and took command of the French army, which, now re-organized and strongly reinforced with men and guns, occupied the French frontier. Immediately in our front were the heights of Vera, which might more properly be called mountains than heights, and were almost perpendicular except on one point, which was strengthened with field-works and redoubts, and might be considered impregnable. The position occupied by the Light Division was a much lower height running along the front.

On the 25th of July 1813, Soult, with sixty thousand

men, forced the pass of Roncesvalles and Maya, and by a variety of skilful operations succeeded in his advance to the neighbourhood of Pampeluna. Our troops were obliged to fall back (fighting), for reinforcements; the union of the 2nd Division, with the 3rd, 4th, 6th and 7th Divisions enabled them to check the enemy's advance in front, while the Light Division moved on his right flank.

General Graham, in the meantime, was obliged to suspend operations at St. Sebastian, and occupy the Bidasso in force. Such was the state of affairs on the 29th of July, 1813. Soult had sent his wounded and artillery back to France, with orders to the latter to go round to the Lower Bidassoa, while he pushed across to St. Sabastian. In attempting this he was severely handled by Lord Wellington, and finding himself in a dilemma, the Light Division having headed him after most fatiguing marches and countermarches amongst these lofty mountains, after which they returned to their old position at Vera.

The Bidassoa had a bend at Vera, from which it ran straight towards the sea for nine miles, after which it turned back to the rear on our left. There was a bridge over it, close to the town of Vera, in which we had a picquet. A few days before the final storming of St. Sebastian, fifty volunteers were called for from each regiment of the 3rd, 4th, and Light Divisions for this service. In the 52nd all were ready to do so, and the seniors were taken. A most gallant attack, which greatly contributed to our establishment in the town, was led by Captain Snodgrass of the 52nd, then serving as Major in the 13th Regiment of Portuguese Infantry, in Bradford's Brigade, which regiment he was in command of. Having ascertained that the inlet of the sea, which flowed under the walls, was fordable at low water, he volunteered to lead the 13th and 24th regiments through it to one of the breaches, which could not be attained in any other way. This was accomplished most gallantly under a murderous fire from the enemy.

While the storming of St. Sebastian was in progress, Soult having collected forty-five thousand men, crossed the Bidassoa by two pontoon bridges on the fords, on the 31st of August, between Vera and the sea, Clausel keeping the Light Division in check with a force at Vera. The latter also managed to establish himself on the other side of the bridge, and endeavoured with Gen. Reille to force their way to St. Sebastian. In this they failed, and were ordered by Soult to retreat; but unfor.. tunately for Clausel, a heavy fall of rain had taken place, commencing at three o'clock which towards night rendered the fords impassible, and broke the pontoon bridges, rendering it impossible for his rear-guard to cross by any other means but the bridge at Vera, of which they managed to obtain possession during the storm which accompanied the rain. Fortunately, although we had been obliged to withdraw our picquet from Vera, there was a fortified house commanding the bridge, under the fire of which the enemy had to defile with fearful loss.

On the 1st September, Lord Beresford having placed a company of the 5th Portuguese Caçadores in Bradford's Brigade at Colonel Colburn's disposal, he gave me the appointment, and I proceeded at once to St. Sebastian to take command of it.

The company consisted of 120 men; one half were armed with rifles, the other half with muskets and bayonets. On my arrival I found it under the fire of the Castle, which still held out, but finally surrendered on the 3rd of September.

The fall of St. Sebastian having enabled Lord Wellington to take the offensive, he took the bold step of crossing the Bidassao, and establishing his left in the strong position occupied by the French right. This was effected in the following manner:—Soult was led to think that the attack would come from the right of our army at Roncesvalles, where there was no obstacle, instead of from the left, where there was a river only passable at low water. Being under this impression, he allowed his troops to be engaged in the construction of field works, at some distance from the mouth of the river. While they were thus engaged Lord Wellington got up his pontoons, and in the night of the 6th of October, in the midst of a violent thunderstorm, collected his troops close to the fords at the mouth of the river.

On the 7th, everything answering, the tents were left

standing to deceive the enemy, and as soon as day broke, our columns moved forward across the fords, driving the enemy before them. At the same time the Light Division, with a division of Spaniards, made their attack on the French position at Vera, and on the mountain between it and the mouth of the river. In this attack the 52nd bore a prominent part under Colonel Colbourn, who commanded the brigade. As I was engaged at the mouth of the river with Bradford's Brigade, I can only say, that having been in position opposite the pass at Vera, from the latter end of June to the 1st September, 1813, I was eye-witness to the field works and redoubts, one above the other, daily erecting by the French, and if any one had told me that it would have been carried as it was, I would have said it was impossible.

CHAPTER V.

Battle of Nivelle — Battles of Nive commenced by author—Retreat of Soult—Passage of the Adour—Investment of Bayonne — Rumours of Peace—Sortie of the Garrison—I am wounded and embark for Oporto—Sail for Ireland, and am Wrecked on the Wicklow coast—Arrival in Dublin—Return to Duty—Battle of Waterloo—Britian in 1798 and in 1816.

At the battle of the Nivelle the French position extended from the source of the Nivelle to its mouth at St. Jean de Luz; the centre, commanded by Clausel, occupied a range of hills on our side of the river, which swept round them from flank to flank. The whole of their position was intrenched and covered with field works, in which the French were busily occupied from the 7th October to the 10th November, the day of the battle. On this occasion the Light Division was engaged with Clausel's right, and succeeded in forcing him from his position. The 52nd bore a very active part, of which I was witness from Bradford's Brigade, which was moved from the coast to the support of their Brigade. Their charge up the hill to attack their entrenchments was very fine. Being sent by General Bradford with an order to the rear, after the action, I was for the first time a witness of camp-followers rifling the dead, and was in some danger from interfering without support.

By this action the way was opened for our advance on Bayonne. My brigade returned to the left wing, now under the command of General Hope, under whom we advanced to Bidart and its neighbourhood.

After the battle of Nivelle, Lord Wellington, from the state of the roads, gave us a month's rest in cantonments; the enemy occupying his intrenched camp in front of Bayonne, from the Adour above the town, to the Adour below the town, which communicated by means of bridges, and having advanced posts extending on the right bank of the Nive to Cambo, where he had a large force.

This was done with equal gallantry, but with great exertion from the state of the roads, which were knee-deep with mud. Our force was twenty-four thousand men, and the Royal road from Bayonne to St. Jean de Luz was better than the cross roads. The Ninth Regiment, led by my company of Caçadores as an advanced guard, were in front. After passing the Mayor of Biarrit's house, I came in contact with the enemy, who occupied a height on the right of the road, and commenced skirmishing with them. This led to a disagreement with the gallant commander of the Ninth who mistook them for Spaniards, and wanted me to cease firing; however, a few minutes convinced him of his error, as several of our men were killed and wounded while we were talking. The enemy soon found it necessary to retire to his entrenched camp, within gunshot of which I occupied a house, and held it till evening. General Bardford's orders were to get my company into fire wherever I could. Acting on this order, by advancing in double time, I got to the head of the column on the Royal road —the Ninth Regiment was the leading regiment of the 5th Division. Gleig, in his "Subaltern," makes the following allusions to this skirmish :—

" The night of the 8th passed quietly over, and I arose about two hours before dawn on the 9th, perfectly fresh and, like those around me, in high spirits. We had been so long idle, that the near prospect of a little fighting, instead of creating gloomy sensations, was viewed with sincere delight; and we took our places, and began our march towards the high-road, in silence, it is true, but with extreme good will. There we remained stationary till the day broke, when, the word being given to advance, we rushed forward in the direction of Bayonne. The brigade to which I belonged took post at the head of the 1st Division, and immediately in the rear of the 5th. This situation afforded to me, on several occasions, as the inequalities placed me, from time to time, on the summit of an eminence, very favourable opportunities of beholding the whole of the warlike mass which was moving; nor is it easy to imagine a more imposing or more elevating spectacle. The entire left wing of the army advanced, in a single continuous column, by the main road, and covered, at the most moderate computation, a space of four miles. As far, indeed, as the eye could reach, nothing was to be seen except swarms of infantry, clothed not only in scarlet, but in green, blue, and brown uniforms; whilst here and there a brigade of four or six guns occupied a vacant space between the last files of one division and the first of another. In rear of all came the cavalry, but of their appearance I was unable accurately to judge, they were so far distant. We had proceeded about five miles, and it was now seven o'clock, when, our advanced guard falling in with the French picquets, a smart skirmish began. It was really a beautiful sight. The enemy made, it is true, no very determined stand, but they gave not up a rood of ground, without exchanging a few shots with their assailants, who pressed forward, vigorously indeed, but with all the caution and circumspection which mark the advance of a skilful skirmisher. The column, in the meanwhile, moved slowly but steadily on, nor was it once called upon, during the whole of the day, to deploy into line."

In the evening we retired to our cantonments, leaving our outposts at the Mayor's house, the Light Division being on its right, with a body of French in their front. During the night of the 9th December, Soult collected sixty thousand men in the intrenched camp on the left bank of the Nive; with this force he advanced at day-break on the morning of the 10th, attacking Campbell's Portuguese Brigade, who occupied the plantations round the Mayor's house.   This post was maintained singly by the latter till our Brigade (which was about two miles in the rear) came to their assistance, the enemy gradually working their way through the wood on our right flank ; we had frequently to retire until they were driven back. On one of these occasions I was running on one side of the hedge, and the French on the other, when my cap fell off—I was doubtful of having time to pick it up, but putting down my hand I got hold of it.   On getting to the end of the hedge, I found our supports coming up, when we returned the compliment, and the enemy had to run back as fast as they had run forward.

Glaig, in his Subaltern (page 172, line 22, and page 173 to line 10), describes this scene :—

"And now the scene of action began to open upon us. We had passed through Bidart,and were descending on the little eminence on which it was built, when the comba-tants became distinguishable : and a very magnificent as well as gratifying spectacle they presented.   The merest handful of British troops were opposing themselves,in the most determined manner, to a mass of men so dence and so extended as to cover the whole of the main road so far as the eye could reach.   Our people were, it is true, giving way; they had already maintained a most unequal contest of upwards of two hours, and their numbers, or-iginally small, were fast deminishing.But no sooner had the head of our column shewn itself than their confidence completely returned, and renewed the struggle with increased alacrity."   For being able to drive them back we were indebted to the gallantry of the 9th Regiment under Colonel Cameron.

My appearance at this time was not very elegant.   I had on a pair of white trowsers (or rather a pair of trow-sers that had been white).   I also wore a pair of new worsted gloves, the blue of which came off most freely on the trowsers, after the heavy showers which we were exposed to, and rendered their appearance rediculous, and as I was a most conspicuous figure, rallying my men, after getting out of the wood, I almost wonder Gleig did not remark it. I have been told that my Lieut.-Colonel St. Clair, who was fond of drawing, drew the scene, introducing me into it, but I did not hear that he introduced the whity blue trowsers.

The fighting continued till dark, when I was ordered to place a chain of communication between the troops on our right and those on our left; in doing this I was obliged to reconnoitre the ground and the position of the enemy, in doing which I was very nearly captured; on my way along our front I could perceive some dark figures on a rising ground in front of a house. Leaving a few men I had with me, at some distance, I advanced and challenged them; the answer was in Portuguese, so I called on one of them to advance, and the answer was, "Come here, you," the Spanish word for 'you' being used instead of the Portuguese word, which satisfied me that it was the enemy I had to deal with. In posting my chain of sentries, we had melancholy evidence of the severity of the action in the number of bodies we had stumbled over; this was the case all through the plantation. Out of 11 officers brought into action, the 5th Caçadores had eight killed and wounded! The proceedings of the Light Division on our right will be found in Napier, vol. vi., pages 379 to 382. On going to General Bradford's quarters in the Mayor's house, I found him with General Hay and a number of field officers; on reporting that I had completed our chain of communication, I had the satisfaction of receiving their thanks for my services on the last two days.

It appears from the above facts that my company of the 5th Caçadores commenced the battles of the Nive, but so little do men know of what is going on around them when engaged, that I was not aware of it until putting my recollections together for this little work.

At day-break on the morning of the 11th, being on the look out for the enemy, I found they had withdrawn from the posts occupied during the night, which I immediately reported to General Bradford, who ordered me to move forward and ascertain what they were about—the General riding with us on a large white horse. We came upon the enemy in great force, who had hidden themselves behind the tank in our front. I at once told General Bradford that they would pick him off, but he continued to expose himself till his horse was shot under him.

By his order I attacked a breastwork in our front, and drove the enemy from it. While doing so I received a blow in the breast from a spent ball. Several of my men heard it strike me, and they called out " The Captain is killed!" in a tone of surprise and sorrow—they appeared to think me invulnerable. I take this opportunity of stating that the soldiers of my company became greatly attached to me, and when I was leaving, after being wounded in the sortie from Bayonne, they actually cried like children. It may appear singular that I should receive such a blow from the spent ball without being wounded, but having the breast of my jacket thickly braided with silk cord, and a silk handkerchief in my breast, the resistance offered by the silk saved me.

The French advancing in force on our right, we were obliged to re-occupy the ridge in front of the Mayor's house, which was attacked in various parts and with various successes till evening, when we still held our ground. The 12th passed off with a heavy cannonade from both sides, which caused considerable havoc.

On the 13th, Soult leaving three Divisions in the entrenched camp in our front, moved the rest of his army to the right bank of the Nive, and attacked Hill, who was placed at great disadvantage. The heavy rain on the 12th had caused his bridge to be carried away, and it took some time to restore it, but he held his ground and finally triumphed. These five days' fighting in which the enemy suffered severely, caused him to retreat behind the Adour, and finally from his entrenched camp at Bayonne.

We re-occupied our cantonments after the battles of the Nive, and had nearly two months' rest before we were again actively employed. On the 23rd February, 1814, Bradford's Brigade having been brought to the front, I was sent with my company to occupy an advanced post close to the entrenched camp at Biarritz, and having posted my sentries within a short distance of the enemy's, without opposition, we made ourselves as comfortable as

circumstances would permit. Shortly after I was ordered
to drive in the enemy, and occupy their post. As they
had allowed me to post my sentries close to theirs, I considered myself bound in honour not to take advantage of
them. I therfore visited mine, and told them to fall back
as soon as I should wave my cap; and having returned
to my post, I ordered the company to fall in, and stepping
forward waved my cap to the enemy's sentries, who took
the hint and retired to their main body, while mine did
the same. We then advanced and continued skirmishing
till evening, when we retired to our former post. We
were relieved by a detachment of Spaniards, and were
moved towards the sea and the entrance of the Adour.
Here we were witness on the 24th of February to the
gallant passage of our gunboats and sailing vessels, prepared by Lord Wellington to form a bridge over the
river. The passage was most difficult, there being a
heavy surf and a bar at the mouth of the river, which was
only passable in one narrow spot. After passing it, the
river suddenly turned to the left, and if a vessel lost her
way she was driven on shore. This occurred in several
instances, and there were several boats and vessels upset
in the passage, and all the crews drowned, with the exception of one midshipman, who was picked up by a gunboat. Unfortunately he was only saved from one death
to undergo another—the gunboat was driven on shore,
and fell on her side—he was thrown out upon the sand,
when the gun fell upon his body and killed him. During
the night of the 23rd and morning of the 24th Colonel
Stopford and six hundred of the Guards passed the river
(eight hundred yards wide and very rapid, running seven
miles an hour at ebb tide) in a raft made of two pontoons;
the rocket battery also passed, which, with the field
battery on our side, repulsed an attack from the garrison
of Bayonne. In the evening the remainder of the 1st
Division and our Brigade crossed on the raft and protected the parties forming the bridge, which was three miles
below Bayonne. This bridge was completed on the 25th.
The first Division and Bradford's Brigade, numbering
eight thousand men, invested the fortress from the Adour
above to the Adour below, the distance being about two
miles; the Spaniards invested the two parts of the en-

trenched camp on the other side of the Adour. The garrison was said to consist of fifteen thousand picked men. On the 27th of February we drove the enemy into the fortress, contracting our investment to half-pistol shot in the centre, which was opposite the citadel, and everything was prepared for a siege. With the exception of a shot from the fortress, (when they could get an object to fire at), nothing particular occurred till the 14th of April, when the enemy made a sortee on our advanced posts at St. Etienne, and succeeded in forcing their way through our troops, killed General Hay, and taking General Hope and Colonel Townsend prisoners. General Hay's wife and daughters had joined him from England a few days before the sortie. General Hinaber with his Germans succeeded in stopping the enemy; in this engagement the 5th Caçadores took an active part.

We occupied a gentleman's country house in rear of the outposts, and having heard the night before of the Peace having been concluded at Paris, the Governor of Bayonne having likewise been informed of it, we retired to rest under the impression that the last shot had been fired—what was our astonishment to be awakened a little before daylight by the enemy's balls flying through our windows. A few minutes found us under arms, and on the left of the Germans, with whom we advanced to the relief of the troops engaged, driving the French into their fortress. Being in command of a wing of the Caçadores, I had them in column in front of the citadel, waiting to see if any further attack would take place, when a ball from the walls wounded one of my men, on which I moved the column behind a house on my left, remaining myself on the look out. Suddenly I felt a blow on the shin, and on looking down found that a ball had enter'd between the two bones, carrying in a piece of the trowsers, which I believe was the last shot fired.

On returning to my quarters I found it occupied as an hospital. General Hay lay dead in the room I had slept in, and General Bradford was under the hands of a surgeon. On seeing me General Bradford ordered the surgeon to stop, and attend to my wound before he finished his dressing.

After writing the above, the manuscript being in the

printer's hands, the following article appeared in the "United Service Magazine" for June, 1859, being part of the "Reminiscences of a Veteran":—

"I was now perfectly recovered, when an order arrived for me to do duty, and take command of the 6th Caçadores in the 2nd Division; so taking leave of my former comrades, I proceeded on my journey. I had a short time before received the arrears of my pay as Major of Brigade, so I had plenty of money. I also escaped from the sortie the garrison made afterwards, and I can conceive from their proximity that the Caçadores must have been roughly handled. Poor Dobbs, after boasting that he had remained uninjured the whole of the war, received on this occasion a wound in the heel, which laid him up for several months."

On seeing this extract, I wrote the editor of the "United Service Magazine" a letter showing that my friend Bunbury was mistaken as to my wound being in the heel, and explaining the part taken by the Caçadores in this affair.

I was sent into quarters in the neighbourhood for the recovery of my wound; the natives showed me as much attention as if I had been their own countryman. After some time I was sent to St. Jean de Luz, where I met with the same kindness. I then embarked for Oporto, where I remained for some time, being billeted on a Portuguese merchant, from whom also I received great kindness. I required this, being actually penniless, although I had six month's pay due to me.

The cause of my being without money was the difficulties raised by their pay office, although I had brought all necessary certificates from the regiment. They are still in my debt the Peninsular prize-money, although trifling, and I have long ceased to look for it. I only got my pay a few days before starting. While at Oporto I was invited to a feast; it was a very disgusting scene. There was a great number of dishes, and almost all the guests made it a point to eat of every dish, and when too full, would go out and get rid of what they had eaten and return to begin a-fresh, while there was Brittons at this time, who acted in the same way with drink. We must give the Portuguese credit for sobriety, except in expectation of a fight, when they would take a pull at their ration rum, and they were surprised when I would not take a "share," telling them that we would do better without it. The officer made no bones in confessing that they had no relish for fighting, and would tell me "You English love fighting!" I said no, but when duty calls we go.

A custom amongst the Portuguese females was that of rougeing while young, they are very well-looking, but when they begin to lose their colour, they commence this foolish habit, which turns them nearly black, except when daubed over with paint.

Being then withdrawn from the Portuguese service by the British Government, I embarked for Dublin in a merchant vessel. In laying in my sea-stock I got a mall cask of port wine which was prepared for the English market, and which, I expected would be such as was in use at home, but I found it anything but palatable being half brandy.

On embarking, I had to leave my Caçador servant behind me, and I cannot help feeling excited whilst I write when I remember his frantic despair at our separation ; he was a reserved silent man, which made it more remarkable. As we sailed up the Irish Channel, our vessel strnck on a rock off the coast of Wicklow, and I landed, and in doing so, one of my crutches broke, and I had to hop over a sandy beach for some distance, whereby I received an injury in the other leg, from which I still suffer. I succeeded in getting a seat in a stage coach to Dublin, and arrived there to the surprise of my friends, who had an évening party. I was rather an uncommon figure for Dublin, my Portuguese uniform and long beard being a new thing there.

I was suffering under my wound for a year, during which time I was promoted to a company in the 52nd, and on Bonaparte escaping from Elba, I found myself able to throw away my crutches, and left Dublin to join the 2nd Battalion of the 52nd, then in Belgium with Lord Wellington, as was also the 1st Battalion.

On reporting myself at the Horse Guards, I received orders to take command of the depot of the 2nd Battallion at Dover, and shortly after joined the skeleton of the

Battalion at Canterbury. The effective men of this
Battallion had been drafted into the 1st Battalion,
which bore a prominent part in the crisis of the battle
of Waterloo.

The iollowing description of this crisis, extracted from
Siborne, vol. ii., chap. 14., pages 176 to 181, will serve
to give an idea of the nature of the combat at the time
when the French were finally forced to give way;—

"Had the second column of attack continued in the
original direction of its advance, it would have come upon
the centre of Adam's Brigade, but having, as it began to
ascend the exterior slope of the main ridge of the Allied
position, slightly diverged to its right, as before observed,
by following the direction of a very gentle hollow, consti-
tuting the re-entering angle, formed by the tongue of
ground that projected from the front of Maitland's Brigade,
and that part of the ridge occupied by Adam's Brigade,
it, in some degree, bent its flank to the latter. This
circumstance was not only observed, but had been in a
great measure anticipated by Lieutenant Colonel Sir
John Colbourn, commanding the 52nd Regiment, an officer of great repute in the British army. He had been
watching with intense anxiety, the progress of the enemy's
column, and, seizing the most favourable moment, he,
without orders, and upon his own responsibility, wheeled
the left company of the 52nd, and then formed the remainder
of the regiment upon that company, for the purpose
of bringing its front nearly paralell with the flank
of the French column. At this moment Adam rode
up and asked Colbourn what he was going to do, to which
the latter replied, ' I o make that column feel our fire.'
Adam, approving of this, ordered Colbourn to move on,
and galloped off to bring up his right regiment, the 71st.
The Duke, who had just seen Maitland's Brigade reformed and posted in the best order, paralell with the
front of the attacking column, was at this moment
stationed on the right of Napier's battery. He despatched
an aide-de-camp (Major the Hon. Henry Percy) to direct
Sir Henry Clinton to advance and attack the Imperial
Guard; but a single glance at Colbourn's forward movement satisfied him that his intention was anticipated; and
he immediately pushed forward the 2nd Battalion, 95th

Regiment, to the left of the 52nd. The head of the French column had by this time nearly reached the brow of the ridge, its front covering almost the whole of Napier's battery, and a portion of the extreme right of Maitland's Brigade. It was still gallantly pressing forward, in defiance of the most galling fire poured into its front by the battery and by the British Guards, when the sudden and imposing appearance of the four-deep line of the 52nd Regiment, bearing directly towards its left flank, in the most admirable and compact order imaginable, caused it to halt. In the next instant, wheeling up its left sections, it opened a rapid and destructive fire from the entire length of its flank against the 52nd Regiment. Colbourn, having brought his line paralell to the flank of the Imperial Guard, also halted, and poured a deadly fire into the mass; and almost at the same moment the rifles of the 2nd Battalion, 95th Regiment, then coming up on the left were levelled and discharged with unerring aim into the more advanced portion of the column. The 71st Regiment was at this time rapidly advancing on the right to complete the Brigade movement. Colburn, eager fully to carry out his projected flank attack upon the enemy's column caused his men to cease firing, and then gave the command, ' Charge ! Charge !' It was answered by three hearty British cheers that rose distinctly above the shouts of ' Vive l'Empereur !' and the now straggling and unsteady fire from the column. The 2nd Battalion, 95th Regiment, hastened to join in the charge on the left. The movement was remarkable for the order, the steadiness, the resolution, and the daring by which it was characterized. The column of the Imperial Guard, which already seemed to reel to and fro under the effect of the front and flank fire, which had been so successfully brought to bear upon it, was evidently in consternation as it beheld the close advance of Adam's Brigade. Some daring spirits—and it contained many within its ranks—still endeavoured to make at least a show of resistance ; but the disorder, which had been rapidly increasing, now became uncontrollable ; and the second column of the Imperial Guard breaking into the wildest confusion, shared the fate of the first, with this difference, however, that in consequence of the combined front and flank fire in which it had been so fatally involved, and of the unrestrained pursuit which deprived it of the power of rallying its component parts, it became so thoroughly disjointed and dispersed, that with the exception of the two rear battalions, which constituted the 1st Regiment of chasseurs (Old Guard), it is extremely doubtful whether any portion of it ever re-united as a regularly formed military body during the brief remaining period of the battle—certainly not on the Allied side of La Belle Alliance, towards which point it directed its retreat. It is necessary to remark that this regiment of the Old Guard, which was commanded by General Cambronne, formed a separate column of support in echelon to, and immediately in the left rear of, the four battalions of the Middle Guard; but so close to each other were the two columns that although an interval was observed between them by Adam's Brigade, when the latter stood in the general front line of the Allied position, they appeared to it as but one column when charged in flank, and may, to all intents and purposes, be considered as having formed one general column of attack; Cambronne's battalions, however, forming the rear of the column, did not become exposed to the fire from Adam's Brigade, inasmuch as neither the 71st Regiment, nor the 3rd Battalion, 95th Regiment, could complete the Brigade flank movement in time to open a fire upon the mass before the actual charge was commenced. Hence, although they turned, along with the rest of the column, yet, unlike the latter, they retained a considerable degree of order."*

The direction to Adam's line, by its right shoulder forward movement having brought it perpendicular to the general front of the French position, that officer became naturally anxious for support upon his right flank, to secure the latter from the enemy's cavalry, which, it was to be presumed, would now be brought forward from his re-

---

*In Siborne's 1st volume, pages 376-7, it will be seen that the British had only 24,000 men and 76 guns, at Waterloo, while the French had 72,000 men, and 246 guns; most of the British allies were worse than useless.

serve. Since none of it had been employed in immediate support of the last attack.

He urgently requested for this purpose the aid of troops from the other part of Clinton's division, and Lieut.-Colonel Halkett, seeing what was required, immediately advanced with the nearest battalion of his Hanoverian Brigade, the Osnabruck bund were in column at quarter distance, and close up in right rear of the 71st Regiment. Thus, Adam's Brigade, maintaining its four deep line, and being flanked by the Hanoverian battalion, which could form squares at any moment, was sufficiently secured against the cavalry.

The confused and disordered mass of the Imperial Guard from the first impulse given it by the flank charge, hastened a short distance in a direction parallel with that of the Anglo-allied line, and then naturally inclining towards the French position, it fell into nearly the same track as that pursued by the first attacking column, viz., towards the first rise of ground intersected by the Charleroi road, a little beyond the Southern extremity of the Orchard of La Haye Saint.

As it approaches the rear of those columns D'Erlons Corps, which had been so desperately opposing Alton's division, it became infected with the panic, and comingled with the flying guard, Adam's Brigade continued its triumphant advance, at first parallel, for a short distance to the Allied line, and then, bringing forward its left shoulders, swept proudly onward in the direction of the French height before mentioned, crowds of fugitives hurrying along, and striving to escape from the pursuing wave that seemed every instant on the point of engulfing them.

During its advance, the front of Adam's Brigade was partially crossed by the squadron of the 23rd Light Dragoons, who was unfortunately fired upon by the 52nd regiment, and it was not until the foremost of them had fallen close upon the bayonets that the error was discovered. Immediately after this incident, a fire of grape was opened upon the 52nd by three French field pieces in the prolongation of its right flank. This infilading of the regiment, in its four-deep line, was a judicious measure on the part of the French artillery, and well calculated to derange the advance of Adam's Brigade. It was, however, very gallantly and speedily checked by the wheeling up and advance of the right section of the 52nd, under Lieutenant Gawber, who succeeded in driving off the guns whilst the rest of the regiment continued the pursuit.

Wellington, as soon as he saw that the success of the charge by Adam's Brigade was so decisive, requested Uxbridge immediately to launch forward some fresh cavalry the probable advance of that of the enemy, and to second the efforts of the infantry in front, by boldly attacking the French reserves which appeared collected in fron. of La Belle Alliance, the critical point of Napoleon's line. Lieut.-Colonel Lord Greenock, Quarter-Master-General of the cavalry, was dispatched to Vivian, with orders for him to move his hussar brigade to its right from its position in rear of Altons division, so as to get clear of their infantry, and then advance directly to the front by the right of Maitland's Brigade of guards. At the same time the Duke turned round to order up the nearest supports to the space which had been vacated in his front line by the advance of Adam's Brigade. But what a spectacle met his view. The three Dutch Belgium squares into which D'Aubrene's Brigade had been formed, and whose unsteadiness, previously described, had greatly augmented as the firing and shouting on the exterior slope of the ridge, of which they could see nothing, became more continuous and intense, were now in a state bordering on dissolution. The faces of the squares were already broken at intervals by groups in the act of abandoning their ranks ; whilst several officers of Vandelure's Brigade, which, as before observed, was drawn up in their rear were zealously exerting themselves to induce these troops to stand fast. The Duke, observing this, called out, "That's right; tell them the French are retiring." This intelligence quickly caught up and spread through their ranks, had the desired effect of restoring them to order. They shortly afterwards formed in columns, and advanced to the front line.

Battle of Waterloo, deducting loss at Quarter-brass.
Siborne, vols, page 460 and 461.

Effective strength of British, 18th June,........21,026
Do.   do. of Germans....................21,851

                                    Total......49,877

Belgians occupied some of these troops, keeping them in their ranks.

Siborne, vol. ii., page 502.

Loss of British, in killed, wounded and missing...6,064
Do. of Germans.............................1,381

The brunt fell on the British, their loss per cent. was 28-8.   Loss of Germans was only 4-7.

I calculate that at this crisis, we had not more than 12,000 effective British, after deducting killed, wounded, and men occupied with the wounded.

It may be satisfactory to compare our circumstances after the battle of Waterloo with the state of affairs in 1798.   At that time Ireland had four hundred thousand inhabitants in open rebellion, and had actually been invaded by a French force; not very large, it is true, but still able to advance unmolested into the interior.   Their conquests on the continent were rapidly progressing; they had a powerful fleet and army under the direction of Bonaparte, a man of first-rate talents, with all the continent under his control.   Against these powers England had to contend single-handed for the greater portion of the time till in 1816, the French fleet had ceased to exist, Bonaparte had been hurled from his dominions, and Great Britain was at peace with all the continental powers, and continued so till the Crimean war, a period of thirty-eight years.

CHAPTER VI.

Reduction of the 2nd Battalion, 52nd Regiment—I am Married—Convinced of my State of Sin—Return to Dublin—An Enquiring Roman Catholic—Numerous Conversions—Ordnance Reforms—I Exchange with Captain Rowan and Settle in Waterford—Jeffry's Song, "Wellington"—There's a Good Time Coming."

After the battle of Waterloo, the 2nd Battalion was reduced, and as I was junior captain, I lost all hopes of active employment. On this I married one of my next door neighbours, whom I had left a child, but found on my return from the Peninsula, a fine young woman. On the evening of my return, we met at my mother's as strangers; she not having been told of my arrival, and I never supposing her to be the child I had left six years before.

On my reduction I returned to Dublin, via Liverpool, and experienced the disadvantage of travelling in those days. After a tedious journey of two days and a night on the top of a coach, I went to a hotel till a packet should be ready to sail; but having become acquainted with a mercantile traveller on the coach, he told me that I might be detained for a week or more, and that my best plan was to take lodgings. I followed his advice and we remained together for a fortnight before I could get a passage, and when we did sail, we only got as far as the Hill of Howth, when we encountered a violent gale, which drove us back to Holyhead, where we were obliged to remain for several days. All my money being spent before I left Liverpool, I was obliged to borrow what I required to bring me over.

Up to this period I was in utter ignorance of my state before God, and the ground of a sinner's hope. The state of the Protestants was lamentable; there was only one clergyman of the Established Church preaching the Gospel in Dublin, and he was silenced as far as the bishop was able. His appointment was from the trustees of the Bethesda; he was not allowed into any other pulpit, nor was any other clergyman allowed into his. The abuse which was lavished upon him by the old card-players and ball-goers led me to respect him, and I occasionally went to hear him; and although his sermons were an hour long, yet they were so well connected that I was never tired of them. The state of society was very bad—drinking, swearing, gambling, duelling, &c., &c., were almost universal.

During a visit to the North of Ireland, I was taken ill at Carrickfergus, where my sister's family was, and while confined to my room, took a book from a shelf to read;

the process of vegetation, as described in it, led me to think of the Great Being who had made all things. About this time a lady directed me to justification by faith in the merits of the Redeemer, and not by our own works ; against this I fought hard.

About this time the Irish Evangelical Society sent a minister to Carrickfergus, and the violent abuse with which he was assailed awakened my curiosity to hear what he had to say, which I found to agree with the Apostolic doctrine. He preached Jesus and the Resurrection—holding Him up as a Prince and a Saivour, exalted to the right hand of God, to give repentance and forgiveness of sins to his people. I became a constant attendant; after some time the duty of "breaking bread," was brought under our notice, which caused me to examine the nature of the Apostolic churches, and led me to unite with the brethren who had thus been brought together in fellowship and breaking of bread. This gave great offence to all my friends, and caused a good deal of ridicule as far as it could be exercised.

On Mr. Flintons first going to Carrickfergus he obtained the use of the Assembly-rooms for preaching in. For some time it was crowded, but there was a general outcry against him from the clergymen of all denominations, and it was taken from him and he was obliged to remove to what was called the old Court-house. This was when I first attended his ministry. In wet weather the rain came in in all directions, still it was considered a great favour to get it, which, if I recollect right, was granted by my cousin, the Rev. R. Dobbs, and who was, at that time, mayor. Under these circumstances it was proposed to build a place of worship; and Mr. Ellis, a gentleman of property in the neighbourhood, gave a site near the castle together with a handsome subscription. This aroused the enemies to perfect rage, and an attempt was made to stop it by claiming the ground as lying waste for the public use.

The attempt failed and the building was commenced under threats of being pulled down as fast as it was built. At last it was roofed in, but whether any foul play had taken place or the foundation was bad, one of the walls gave way, and there was a great shout of joy from those who wished it down, while the friends of its erection were nearly in despair; it was, however, finished and occupied. The little church formed, and bread was broken in it.

About this time the 43rd Regiment was quartered in Belfast, and our Captain Maddens, brother, was detached to Carrickfergus. It was he who was supposed to be mortally wounded in the ditch at Badajos. When his brother was killed, it was he who sought a copy of the Scriptures but could not get it. While dining with him at a clergyman's house in Carrickfergus, I heard so much ridicule of Mr. Flinton and his congregation that I got up and left the room—this led Madden to attend our meeting. After he had recovered from his wound at Badajos he relapsed into his former careless state, but just before his visit to Carrickfergus he had attended the death of a favourite brother of the 95th Regiment at Liverpool, which was the means of awakening him permanently, and he has since become a clergyman in the establishment.

My old prisoner, Major Kelly, also was detached to Carrickfergus from Belfast, and a few years since having paid a visit to my friends in the North, I was with my brother-in-law at Cusnendall and strolled into a tower where they kept prisoners, when in conversation with the keeper—an old pensioner—I asked him what regiment he belonged to? His answer was the 11th, on which I asked him if he knew Major Kelly? His reply was that he was his servant, and was often with him on his reconnoitering parties, but on the occasion I met Major O Kelly it was unsafe to take him with him.

I have now the happiness of finding almost all the members of my family taking more or less active parts in the cause of truth, some in India, others in America, and many at home. It has also been a privilege to have my simple testimony to the Saviour bearing fruit, of which I was not aware for years after the seed was sown.

Having returned to Dublin, I was shortly after married, and went to reside in Carrickfergus, where I remained till 1823, when the Duke of Wellington having been appointed Master-General of the Ordnance, gave me the Barrack-mastership of Nenagh, in the county of Tipperary. Before leaving Carrickfergus I had seen every house supplied with the scriptures, and left a school under the Kildare Street Society at full work. This barrack district comprised some of the worst parts of Galway, Clare, Limerick, and Tipperary. Whilst on this service, I was privileged to give my assistance to the London Hibernian School Society, the Evangelical, Bible, and some other Societies, having the same objects in view, by which some thousand copies of the Scriptures passed through my hands. On one occasion a lady in the neighbourhood sent me an enquiring Roman Catholic who had got possession of a Bible. In conversation I happened to show him the nature of the primitive churches, and the fellowship that should exist among its members. He said "I have been looking for that for some time, and I'll join you."

Accordingly Doctor Townley, the Independent minister of Limerick, (whose private income carried on the work he was engaged in) having come over to Nenagh, Daniel Moran, Miss Molloy and myself broke bread with him, in a cabin which I had fitted up as a place of worship. This beginning resulted in a number of converts from the Church of Rome, and an awakening among the Protestants, and the formation of small churches of a similar nature at Castletown, Borris-o-Kane, and at Leap Castle, which afterwards was the origin of what are now called the Plymouth Brethren. The revivals in the North of Ireland at the present moment, 1859, have drawn to my recollection a remarkable instance of the deep conviction which a Protestant friend of mine underwent; he laboured for some time under similar depression, but when he saw clearly the remedy in the Gospel, met with similar relief; he was brother to one of the first members of our little church, but shortly after died rejoicing in the Saviour. These Christian brethren have been scattered abroad, but I have been occasionally gratified by hearing of their stedfastness in the Faith; I have also found that the Scriptures which passed through my hands have been treasured by many who did not dare to make an open profession.

The following instance of the effect produced by reading the Scriptures gave me great satisfaction :—Having taken shelter in a cabin one day from a heavy shower of rain, I found an old man sitting by the fire, as usual, he offered me a seat and I sat down, and we got into chat, first on general subjects, and afterwards on Scriptural truths, with which he was greatly interested, on which I asked him if he would like to have a Testament, he said he would, so I sent him one by Daniel Moran, he kept it for about two month's, and was reading it almost day and night, at which his friends became greatly alarmed and called in the priest, who wanted him to burn it, he said he would do no such thing, but for peace-sake he would return it to the gentleman who gave it to him, he accordingly gave it to Moran who generally passed his door on his way to Nenagh--to bring it back to me, telling Moran his reasons. Some time after doing so, being in a dying state he requested his neighbour, Mr. Dungan of Nigh, to assist him in making his will, which led to a conversation on his hopes of salvation, which he declared to be, on the Saviour, to the exclusion of all creatures. On Mr. Dungan asking him how he came to this conclusion, he said, by reading a Testament given him by a gentleman, but, said Mr. Dungan, Captain Dobbs told me you only kept it a short time. " Short time as it was said he, I found there was only one Saviour in it."

About the time that the above circumstance occurred I happened to visit my friends in Dublin, and heard that a christian friend and neighbour was in the last stage of water on the chest. Every year she had been in the habit of sending me a little christian remembrance, but I had no idea that there was anything more meant by it. On this occasion she expressed a wish to see me, and I found her gasping for breath. She said, John, you were the first to speak to me of Jesus."

The Ordnance Department, particularly the Barrack Department, was full of abuses when it came into the hands of the Duke, from which, when I left in 1841, it was almost clear.

One article of barrack accommodation compared with the present period, will give an idea of the difference. Most of the barracks were houses hired for the purpose, having a number of low, small rooms. The permanent barracks had larger ones, but all were filled with double wooden bedsteads, touching each other, which contained four men, two above and two below, and the crevices of the wood were full of bugs.

One instance will show the system of abuse which prevailed up to the Duke's time. Coals were kept in large open yards, and issued by measure, and the barrack-master was allowed to charge a certain proportion for waste. The fact was, however, that a large surplus arose from the slaking of the coals. Under the new system the public get credit for every pound surplus, so that the saving is very great indeed.

My district at Nenagh was a lawless one, and at times my visits to out-stations, which were numerous, were frequently attended with personal danger; daily murders were committed, and in the year 1825 Pastorini's prophecy was expected to be fulfilled by a universal massacre of Protestants, and immense collections of people marched through the country, with green sashes, and banners flying, moving in perfect order, in sections, with a large body of mounted men, acting as cavalry. While preparing my little place of worship, they marched past it, Daniel Moran, who was a mason by trade, being at the time engaged in the work, but his faith was strong, and he remained unmoved. Previous to his conversion Moran was the leader of a large faction which had regular pitched battles at Borrisokane. On one occasion, his party being inferior in number to his adversaries, he made them take off their coats, saying that it would prevent any one going away—his party gained the victory. He manifested the same boldness in his Christian course by bearing the reproaches and attacks of his friends and neighbours, many of whom afterwards adopted his views; he had four brothers and one sister who with their families joined him and his family; the children were as bold as their parents.

In visiting one of my out-stations—Tomgrany—at the other side of the Shannon and in the County Galway I had an opportunity of seeing the dreadful consequences of the old Tythe system. There being no inn in the village, I was requested by the clergyman to take a bed at his Glebe, which was a short distance from the village. After visiting the barrack I believe I dined with the officer in command, and at dusk proceeded to my night quarters. On arriving at the hall-door and rapping I heard dogs barking and a great bustle inside from whence I was challenged, and on giving a satisfactory answer the door was opened by one man whilst another stood opposite it ready to shoot me if an enemy. On entering the dining room I found the windows which were on the ground floor barracaded with thick sheets of iron. It appears that the Tythes were collected with great severity, and things tithed which was not customary in other parishes; the consequence was that the people endeavoured to shoot the clergyman, firing into his windows and lying in wait for him as he went out, which he never did without an armed man on each side of the road and himself armed with several braces of pistols. He had several narrow escapes and was once desperately wounded.

I had another station in the same county—Mount Shannon. It was a Protestant colony—they were palatines, and I often got myself ferried across to Cameron fort, another of my out-stations, on the Tipperary side. Onone occasion during political excitement, I left Mount Shannon on foot, for the ferry, and had to pass through a number of potatoe diggers to the river, they allowed me to go half way before they began the most hideous shouting and yelling I ever heard before or after. I was alone, but armed with a brace of pistols, it at once struck me that if I proceeded to the river the boatmen might not be willing to put me across, however, my anxiety to get home turned the balance and I proceeded without taking any notice of their noise, and the ferrymen making no difficulty, I passed the river in safety.

On another occasion when crossing from Youghal, on the Nenagh side, to Tomgrany, in Galway, with my ferryman Shawn Baun, and his sister, who pulled one of the oars, the boat a very old one sprung a leak when half way across—the passage was about five miles—his sister a very pretty girl, and when boating bare legged, with the most perfect unconcern thrust her toe into the hole, which, with my assistance baling got us across in safety.

The murders and attempts at murder were of constant occurrence. On one of my visits to my station at Cameron Fort, I found a Mr. Minchin had been murdered the night before; he was thrown into the river, and the time of his murder discovered by the stoppage of his watch. It was said that it was by persons whom he had detected robbing him. If this was the case it was singular that the watch was not taken.

Another murder was perpetrated on the high road, close to Toomavara, another of my out-stations, on the Dublin road. It was at noon day, in sight of the chapel, with the congregation just coming out, who were witnesses of the deed, but made no effort to arrest the perpetrator. It was under suspicion that he had given information of some political affair.

Various attempts were made to shoot my friend Capt. Garvey. He was agent to Lord Bloomfield and Lord Norbury, and was constantly receiving threatening letters, and on several occasions fired at; on one, Mrs. Garvey was sitting beside him in his gig, close at their own gate, when he was fired at from behind a hedge at the side of the road, the ball passed him and struck Mrs. Garvey's bonnet, hurting her with a piece of the wire.

I received some threats myself, but they were never put into execution, which was rather singular, as one of the Roman Catholic clergy called Therry used to make very free with my name, he was considered a great orator, and used to commit his sermons to memory, in so doing he used to walk up and down the garden of a gentleman who lived some doors above my house in Barrack-street, where he supposed himself unseen, and was able to practice his action as well as his speech, the latter was generally violent, but when he wished to turn any one into ridicule, he selected such titles as the following:—He called me the "Carrickfergus ruffian," Miss Cambridge, "the petticoat angel," Mrs. Falkner, the Protestant curate's wife, who wore glasses, "the four-eyed hypocrite," &c.,

While living in the street I was near committing a murder myself. One evening while Mrs. Dobbs and myself were sitting at the fire, we heard a rap at the door, then a scream from our housemaid, and a rush of persons into the hall, I snatched up the poker and rushed out, when I saw the maid lying on the stairs, and an immense tall figure just before me, with a crowd of persons behind it, on which I made a blow at its head, which knocked it to pieces and caused a general retreat, it was a person dressed up to represent St. Bridget, and I only struck a broom elevated on a pole.

As I am about it, I may as well give a ghost story of the same locality. The house I lived in was a large one, and for some time various were the reports brought me by the servants and others, that every night the step of a person ascending and descending the stairs was heard, I could not make out what it was, till at last, a circumstance occurred which led me to suspect it was a rat, and I accordingly watched, and finding it was so, followed it down to the kitchen and got it behind the door, but it escaped at the opening. It was shortly afterwards killed by a young kitten, and we had no more ghosts. It was a very large rat, and the manner they light on their four legs on steps of stairs is exactly like a footstep.

My family having increased to eleven children, I thought it would be for their interest to have the price of my commission, so I sold out, and invested the money in the Agricultural Bank, the failure of which and my reduced income placed me in difficulties which gave me some trouble to surmount; about this time, 1841, Captain Rowan, Manager of the Waterford District Lunatic Asylum, asked me to exchange with him, which I agreed to do, he managing matters with the Duke and Lord Lieutenant, so that I had no trouble in the matter.

In the year 1848, being the fiftieth year since the Rebellion of 1798, there was an attempt at outbreak in Ireland, in which the R. C. Chaplain of this Asylum was deeply implicated, and having gone to join the insurgents at Ballingarry, in laymans attire, was taken up in mistake for Dillon, one of the rebel leaders. Doctor Wm. Connolly, our Visiting Physician, having expressed his disapprobation of their proceeding, he was told by the chaplain that he should have the first shot. All the loyal inhabitants of Waterford were sworn in Special Constables, I amongst the rest, and we were about forming ourselves into a corps for mutual defence when the overthrow at Ballingarry rendered it unnecessary. On the evening of the outbreak there was a report that the troops which had been withdrawn from Waterford with the exception of the pensioners who were left in charge of the barracks, had been defeated, and almost the whole population were gathered on the Quay, I amongst the rest waiting for the mail, by which the news was expected. From the way in which I was eyed, I have little doubt thefe would have been an outbreak that night if the report had proved true. Pikes had been prepared, paterns having been distributed amongst the people, one of which is in my possession.

Having conducted the duties of the asylum with diligence I have the satisfaction to find that it is not inferior to any other Asylum in the United Kingdom, the recoveries being as numerous and the expenditure less than those with which I have had an opportunity of comparing it..

And now I leave it in 1863 on the most friendly terms with the officers of the institution, who, with the attendants of all classes, have evidenced unfeigned regret at my retirement. I have also to acknowledge the kindness of Board of Governors and the Members of the County and City Grand Jury, with whom I have been brought into contact from time to time.

Having been in the public service 57 years, I am now desirious of freedom from the cares of official life.

My recollections of the two great men, Nelson and Wellington, who have passed away during the period referred to in this book are fully described in Jeffry's song of "Wellington."

Having now glanced over the past sixty years, I look forward with confidence to the future. My hopes are founded on the gracious Revelation of the Almighty. To his servants Daniel and Isaiah, the former giving an outline of the history from his own time to the end of the world, the greater part fulfilled and the latter in his 2nd chapter, 2 to 4 verses describing the thousand years which are to proceed the General Judgment (see Revelation, chapter xx:,) which may be summed up, as regards war, in the two first verses of Russell's popular song: "There's a good Time Coming."

"THERE'S A GOOD TIME COMING, BOYS."

I.

There's a good time coming, boys,
   A good time coming ;
We may not live to see the day,
But earth *shall* glisten in the ray,
   Of the good time coming
Cannon balls may aid the truth,
   But thought's a weapon stronger,
We'll win our battle by its aid—
   Wait a little longer.

II.

There's a good time coming, boys,
   A good time coming,
War in all men's eyes shall be
A monster of iniquity
   In the good time coming ;
Nations shall not quarrel then,
   To prove which is the stronger,
Nor slaughter men for glory's sake—
   Wait a little longer.

DAWNING OF THE GOOD TIME.

The following extracts from Polehamptons Memoirs show how it has began in the 52nd regiment, and from the Scripture Readers and Soldiers Friend Society's report in other regiments also :—

MEMOIRS OF THE REV. N. S. POLEHAMPTON.

In his description of his work at Lucknow, 1857, he says, page 92. "Now we come to the barracks; two immense squares, with low buildings all around them, formerly the king of Oude's stables, now the barracks for the private soldiers of the 52nd Queens', and not bad ones either. The men are just being formed into two companies of one hundred each; about three hundred march off to the Roman Catholic chapel, the rest are marched up to a number of forms put ready for them, just outside the hospital, in the open air."

Page 33.—I also go on Thursday night, at the same time, to the same place, and preside at a prayer meeting, which about fifty men attend. They hold it every night; one of them reads the Bible and expounds it, and one night they have extempore prayer, and on the other the prayers of the Church of England. The meeting is composed of churchmen and dissenters; there is only one officer who comes, the Quarter-master. It is very gratifying, and very surprising, considering what ones impression of soldiers in general are, to find so much genuine piety as there undoubtedly is among them. Last Thursday was my first night of going to them; it reminded me so much of my Capthorn lecture! there were quite fifty men.

Page 16.—"It has gratified me much to find these men in several cases, when I have been talking to them on their sick and sometimes dying bed, reminding me of things which I said in sermons; in one case, several weeks before. Two of the little band of fifty, who have a nightly prayer meeting, have died; and the contrast between the manner in which these and some of the other men have met death very striking."

HIS FAREWELL SERMON TO 52ND.

Page 4.—"Be not only soldiers, but good soldiers of Jesus Christ; with many such so far as man can judge, I have met in this regiment, I pray that you, my brethren, may be kept steadfast in the course upon which you have entered. All those who will endeavour to serve Christ faithfully must encounter opposition, and ridicule, and sneers wherever they may be placed."

Such has been my experience for the last fifty years, but I have been comforted by receiving the right hand of fellowship from many christian friends, male and female, Churchmen and Dissenters. When I was first added to the church of Christ the number was very small, but blessed be God for having greatly increased them, and they are bearing a faithful witness in every part of the globe to the written witness, now so freely circulated amongst its inhabitants.

By a letter from Sealhote of the 11th July, 1860, there appears to be a great increase of believers in the 52nd and the other troops quartered with them as well as civilians, 22 officers and gentlemen having been counted at their prayer meeting.

In conclusion, I think it will be encouraging to glance at the state of God's written and living witnesses from the time they lay dead in the great city in 1216, and the period of my own observations. I take Sismondi a Roman Catholic writer for their death in 1216, at which time the art of printing had not been discovered. He says in page 115:—" We have thus traced the total extinction of the first reformation—the slaughter had been so prodigious—the massacres so universal—the terror so profound, and of so long duration that the church appeared to have completely attained her object. The worship of the reformed Albigenses had every where ceased. All teaching was become impossible. Almost all the doctors of the new church had perished in a frightful manner, and the very small number of those who had succeeded in escaping the crusaders, had sought an Asylum in the most distant regions, and were able to avoid new persecutions only by preserving the most absolute silence respecting the doctrines and their past history. The private believers, who had not perished by the fire and the sword, or who had not withdrawn by flight from the scrutiny of the inquisition, knew that they could only save their lives by burying their secret in their own bosoms.—For there were no more sermons, no more prayers, no more christian communion, no more instruction; even their children were not made acquainted with their secret sentiments."

I now refer to my own recollections of their state in 1815, the year of the battle of Waterloo, and the commencement of 1860, when the bishop of Rome has lost his three kingdoms.

Bibles in 1216 were all in manuscript and very few in number, in 1815 they had been increased by printing, but very few still, all had the Apocryphal books attached to them. The Bible Society was in its infancy, and was opposed by all the bishops and most of the established clergy; the few that gave it support were scoffed at and treated as heretics; if such was the case in England and Ireland what must be the state of the rest of the world have been.

Bibles in 1860 have found their way into every part of the habitable globe; steam-presses are multiplying copies whilst a multiplicity of agencies are circulating them.

STATE OF THE LIVING TESTIMONY.

God's people were few in 1815. They, as well as the written testimony, had to prophesy still in sackcloth. In 1860 we find them in every nation and in all classes, so that the folly of those who have caused the Written Testimony to be evil spoken of, is becoming daily more manifest by the increase of the living testimony; and the "great mystery of iniquity" which began to work while the Apostles were yet alive, and gradually extended itself, mixing truth and error so cunningly together that if it were possible, the elect of God themselves would have been deceived; but it pleased God to preserve His witnesses through their 1260 years of trials, and while he who has worn the triple crown, as fortold by Daniel, had subjected all the earth to his rule, a remnant of faithful men in the valleys of Piedmont, a short distance from his capital, were preserved to testify against his usurpations. These people were slaughtered in numbers, and in many instances flying for their lives carried with them the message of mercy, which has gradually been extending itself to the present moment.

The present circumstances of the Abigenses speaks volumes from being persecuted to the death (as described by Sismonde); they are now permitted the unrestricted exercise of their religion.

That an effort on the part of Satan's emissaries should take place was to be expected, and whilst Evangelical truth is extending on the one hand, by which sacrificing priests, creature mediators, bodily exercises, and justification by works are overthrown, the Roman Catholic and Puseite systems are labouring to subvert it by restoring the errors which have been only partially protested against by some of the reformed systems.

Paganism has also received some deadly blows in India and China, while Mahomatanism is gradually drying up, leaving a vacuum to be filled up by Christianity, Under these circumstances what are the people of God called on to do? To have the praises of God in their mouths and the two-edged sword (the scriptures) in their hands, which, under God's blessing, will overthrow by the spirit of his mouth not only the "mystery of iniquity" but all systems of error make manifest the folly of those who have caused the way of truth to be evil spoken of and render war unnecessary by removing the cause of it. And should it please God to spare me for a few years more, I expect to see the vast expenditure now lavished on war, on false religion and folly, applied to the propagation of truth and the removing of the burthens under which all nations are suffering more or less.

THE END.

The two following papers being the result of forty-seven years thought on natural and revealed religion, I annex for public consideration.

PLAIN FACTS FOR PLAIN PEOPLE.

The human mind is lost in the consideration that all things had a beginning, and that they owe their existence to a great first cause.

The part of the creation which particularly engages our attention is the earth we inhabit and the heavenly bodies by which it is surrounded, the materials of which it is formed, the animated nature by which it is inhabited, and the changes it has undergone.

Of the space by which we are surrounded we may form a faint idea, from facts ascertained by scientific men, one of which, that from the most distant star, which our eye, assisted by powerful glasses can reach, a ray of light takes 10,000 of our years to reach the earth, while the Nebula consists of a multitude of stars, the individuality of which are unobservable.

Natural religion directs us to a great first cause, but we are privileged in having a direct revelation from Himself, through the agency of our fellow men, inspired by the Holy Ghost for the purpose. Of these Moses appears to be the leader, although it is supposed that the book of Job was written before his time.

Moses informs us that all things were made by God, agreeing with the conclusion arrived at by natural religion, but giving us a name for the great first cause, while other portions of the scripture reveal Him in three persons—Father, Son, and Holy Ghost.

Moses describes the state of the earth at the beginning of the year one, of our time, as being without form and void, and in a state of darkness over deep waters.

He then states that the spirit of God moved upon the waters, producing light, which, changing with darkness, became the 1st day.

On the second day God produced a firmament from the midst of the waters. The expansion produced carrying up with it an immense body of the water which had been covering the earth.

On the third day the quantity of water removed from the earth by the firmament left a large portion of it uncovered, which was called land, and the water remaining, sea. God then caused the earth to bring forth the vegitable kingdom, each species having its seed within itself.

On the fourth day God prepared two great light bearers, one to give light by day, the other to reflect its light by night. The relative position of the earth and sun, now causes the day and night, summer and winter, seed time and harvest; while the relative position of the earth and moon by their attraction and reflection causes the ebb and flow of the tide.

On the fifth day God caused the water to bring forth abundantly, birds to fly in the air, and fishes to swim in the sea.

On the sixth day God caused the earth to bring forth living creatures after their kind, and made or created Man in his own image or likeness.

On the seventh day God rested from his labours, and set that portion of time apart for man's service to him, but the work of redemption being finished by the resurrection of our Lord Jesus Christ on the first day of the week, it is now called the Lord's day, and observed by His followers instead of the seventh day. On that day they show forth their faith in his atonement by the breaking of bread.

Of the change or changes the earth has undergone between its first creation and its reformation during the six days recorded by Moses, we have no means of judging more than that animal remains are constantly found which had no existence on the surface of the present earth, which leads to the certainty that it had been inhabited by a race or races of animals now extinct, and by analogy with a full supply of vegetable food for their support, which, by the various convulsions of the crust of the earth's surface, have been engulphed, and form by their decay beds of coal and pools of oil now so abundant. And it is to be particularly remarked that there are no fossil remains of man previous to the six days recorded by Moses, and that while the language employed for the other parts of God's six days labour is to cause the thing to take place from matter already in existence; with regard to man, it was a thing altogether new.

We have now to consider another order of created beings—Angels, their nature superior to man. From the scriptures we find that a portion of the angelic host rebelled against their maker, and were expelled from his presence, but allowed to exercise a free agency (with the exception of 1,000 years restraint) till the general judgment of men and angels shall assign them to their final punishment.

Satan, the leader of this rebellion, having been allowed to use his free agency on man—also a free agent—tempted him to his fall, by which he lost the image and likeness of God, became spiritually dead in trespasses and sin, and the sentence of death was passed upon him.

That this fall was foreknown and provided for before it took place, is plainly taught in scripture, God being pleased to devise a plan by which he could be just and yet the justifier of a people to be saved out of his rebellious creatures. This has been done by his taking our nature in the womb of a virgin and suffering as man the punishment due to man's sins, while as God he rose from the dead, having all power in heaven and earth, sending forth the Holy Ghost he makes a people willing, forgives them their sins and commences a work of sanctification in them, which is shown by their testimony to the truth and a walk and conversation becoming his gospel, they being kept by the power of God through faith unto salvation, to be revealed in the last time, each being born again of the incorruptable seed of the Word of God, which liveth and abideth for ever, thus fulfilling the prophetic declaration of God that the seed of the woman (our Lord Jesus Christ) should bruise the serpent's head, while in doing so he should suffer himself; also, that there should be enmity between the two races, and we find it commence in Adam's two sons,—Able offering the sacrifice of faith in a dying Saviour was accepted; while Cain rejecting the atonement himself, became jealous of the favour granted to his brother and killed him.

Although a few instances of faithful men amongst the Antediluvians are recorded, the bulk of mankind became so depraved that it pleased God to destroy every living creature on the face of the earth, by overflowing it with water, as at the commencement of his six days' labour, with the exception of Noah and his family, who were preserved in a large wooden vessel, prepared by him amidst the jeers and scoffs of his fellow men.

This great overflow of water was caused by the breaking up of the bottom of the sea, and the discharge of the water suspended in the atmosphere, this water having been absorbed by the air, and the fountains of the deep stopped, we find, in various parts of the land left dry, thick masses of shells, some of them on the tops of mountains.

From Noah's three sons we can trace the various nations now in existence; also the genealogy of the Saviour from the Virgin Mary, through David, Judah, Isaac, Abraham, and Shem, as foretold by inspired writers, Abraham standing pre-eminent as the father of the faithful.

To Jacob's posterity, the inspired writings of the Old Testament were committed and preserved to the coming of the Saviour, and then with the Apostolic writings called the New Testament, by his Disciples, to the present moment, in the face of the followers of satan who have endeavoured to destroy, corrupt, and by causing it to be evil spoken of, prevent its being read or circulated, for which they have good reason, as it is the instrument for exposing their folly.

The Apostle Peter tells in his second letter that as the ungodly were destroyed in the days of Noah by water, so satan, being liberated from restraint, should raise up a host of scoffers at the end of the thousand years who shall be burnt to death by fire so intense as to melt the elements of which the earth and air is composed; from which Christ's faithful followers are preserved; being caught up while still alive to meet Him in the air, when coming with the remainder of his elect people to hold the general judgment on good and bad, all undergoing a resurrection of the body.

After these stupendous events we are authorized to look for a new heaven and a new earth, prepared by

Christ for his people, where none of the evils which have existed on this earth will be permitted; where all distinction of sex, sects, or nation, shall cease; no more deaths, sorrows, or strife, amongst its inhabitants who have bodies like unto Christ's glorified body, and where they shall for ever enjoy His personal presence.

CHRISTIAN FELLOWSHIP.

As soon as an individual finds on self-examination that he has passed, by a change of mind, from natural to revealed religion, termed by the Saviour as being born again, a change wrought by the Holy Ghost, whereby they are enabled to call the Great First Cause, Abba or Father, through the mediation of his Son, our Lord Jesus Christ. He or she should seek union with the rest of the family located in the neighbourhood; if they have not yet been baptized with water, they should get a baptized member to do so in the name of the Father, Son, and Holy Ghost.

Such society evidencing their decipleship by continuing in the Apostles Doctrine, fellowship with one another, breaking bread together, to show forth their Lord's death until he come, and offering prayer and thanksgiving to God for all mankind.

Their public worship should be conducted without disorder or confusion, the men being allowed to address the meeting in course, but the number at each service not to exceed three; their words should be few, and well ordered, so that the assembly may be edified, but not wearied. The prayers should be short, simple, and to the purpose.

The society should choose from amongst themselves a ruling elder, bishop, or overseer, whose office it shall be to preside and direct the proceedings, and be responsible for the order of the meeting, as it regards teaching.

If the number of members require it, deacons and deaconnesses should be appointed to attend the wants of the poor brethern, and provide suitable accommodation for public worship.

It is the duty and privilege of a Christian to make known the glad tidings proclaimed by the Gospel to their neighbours, whose minds remain unchanged, and to contribute to the support of Evangilists, or Missionaries who go forth to a distance for the purpose.

Waterford, 10th June, 1863.   J. D.

Also published in facsimile in *The Spellmount Library of Military History* and available from all good bookshops. In case of difficulty, please contact Spellmount Publishers (01580 893730).

HAMILTON'S CAMPAIGN WITH MOORE AND WELLINGTON DURING THE PENINSULAR WAR by Sergeant Anthony Hamilton
Introduction by James Colquhoun
Anthony Hamilton served as a Sergeant in the 43rd Regiment of Foot, later the Oxford and Buckinghamshire Light Infantry. He fought at Vimiero and took part in the retreat to Corunna, vividly describing the appalling conditions and the breakdown of the morale of the British Army. He subsequently fought at Talavera, Busaco, the Coa, Sabugal, Fuentes de Oñoro, Salamanca and Vittoria. He also volunteered to take part in the storming parties of the sieges of Ciudad Rodrigo and Badajoz. During these actions, he was wounded three times.
Published privately in New York in 1847, this rare and fascinating account has never before been published in the United Kingdom.

RANDOM SHOTS FROM A RIFLEMAN by Captain John Kincaid
Introduction by Ian Fletcher
Originally published in 1835, this was the author's follow-up to *Adventures in the Rifle Brigade* – and is a collection of highly amusing, entertaining and informative anecdotes set against the background of the Peninsular War and Waterloo campaign.

RECOLLECTIONS OF THE PENINSULA by Moyle Sherer
Introduction by Philip Haythornthwaite
Reissued more than 170 years after its first publication, this is one of the acknowledged classic accounts of the Peninsular War. Moyle Sherer, described by a comrade as 'a gentleman, a scholar, an author and a most zealous soldier', had a keen eye for observation and an ability to describe both the battles – Busaco, Albuera, Arroyo dos Molinos, Vittoria and the Pyrenees – and the emotions he felt at the time with uncommon clarity.

ROUGH NOTES OF SEVEN CAMPAIGNS: in Portugal, Spain, France and America during the Years 1809–1815 by John Spencer Cooper
Introduction by Ian Fletcher
Originally published in 1869, this is one of the most sought-after volumes of Peninsular War reminiscences. A vivid account of the greatest battles and sieges of the war including Talavera, Busaco, Albuera, Ciudad Rodrigo, Badajoz, Vittoria, the Pyrenees, Orthes and Toulouse and the New Orleans campaign of 1815.

For a free catalogue, telephone
Spellmount Publishers on

01580 893730

or write to

The Old Rectory

Staplehurst

Kent TN12 0AZ

United Kingdom

(Facsimile 01580 893731)

(e-mail enquiries@spellmount.com)

(Website www.spellmount.com)